The author is an Irish female with a passion for writing from an early age. Married to Declan, the love of her life. She is living in Galway city, in the heart of the Claddagh. Already a published author with a love of fiction, she has dedicated her life to writing. Her main ambition is to bring joy to the reader.

I would like to dedicate this book to my dad, Martin Finnerty. Endeared to all due to his gentle and caring ways. In life, a dear and trusted friend, in death, a terrible loss. Dependable, compassionate, emphatic, honest, and loving. That was the man that I saw in my dad. This one's for you, Dad.

Mary Finnerty-Morris

Before the Fog

Austin Macauley Publishers™
London • Cambridge • New York • Sharjah

A CIP catalogue record for this title is available from the British Library.

ISBN 9781528913416 (Paperback)
ISBN 9781528913423 (ePub e-book)

www.austinmacauley.com

First Published (2021)
Austin Macauley Publishers Ltd
25 Canada Square
Canary Wharf
London
E14 5LQ

Chapter 1

As Lizzie sat under the hair dryer, the words went round in her head, "Your husband has Alzheimer's."

Retired now, from a long career in nursing, she knew the prognosis.

She watched as the young hairdressers buzzed around the salon, oblivious to what was tormenting her mind. She couldn't hear the chatter with the hair dryer buzzing away in her ears but she could see the carefree expressions on their faces, and rightly so. They were young, alive, and joyous as one is in youth.

She, too, had enjoyed her young days she recalled, could gallivant with the best of them, had seen many groggy mornings too after the night before, yes, those were the days alright. Not a care in the world.

Francis was a handsome young soldier who had swept her off her feet at first sight, tall and ever so smart-looking in his uniform, she had fallen head over heels before he had spoken to her at all.

She had spent her rent money on a new frock she'd spotted in the window of the only ladies' shop in the town. It was beautiful and she had to have it. She would tell her landlady she'd lost her wages and would catch up on the rent the following week (It was only a white lie!).

It was green with white polka dots, she remembered it to this day.

She would wear it to the dance on Saturday night, with her white slingback sandals and her white patent handbag. She could hardly wait.

She'd felt like a film star that night, had washed her hair and gone to the hairdressers to have it blow dried as was done in those days, was much cheaper than having a whole hairdo.

Francis was standing with his soldier friends at the entrance to the dance hall, not a fancy hall by any means of the word. Had to walk through muck to get there. It was in the middle of a big field and if it rained at all, sure you will have muck up to your ankles.

Of course it had rained nonstop that day, she remembered, had to run to the makeshift powder room to wipe off her sandals.

Just as she approached the entrance to the hall with Maisie tagging behind as usual, a shy sort never wanted to be the first to go in the door, she'd caught a glimpse of Francis.

Much taller than the others, he sort of stood out. Though all four boys looked quite handsome in uniform, there was something about Francis. "Are you alright there, Lizzie?" The hairdressing assistant lifted the flap on the hairdryer.

"I'm okay lovey." Lizzie smiled and off she went about her business, leaving Lizzie to her thoughts.

She had danced the night away with Maisie, laughed her heart out and twirled about in her new frock to her heart's content.

Wonderful memories.

She'd watched Francis from the dance floor and wished he might ask her to dance. It was coming near the end of the night, early hours of the morning in fact, as was usual back then. It was often four and five in the morning before they got home, *different times!*

Maisie had gone to powder her nose when Lizzie got a tap on her shoulder, "Care to dance?"

Her knees felt wobbly, she recalled and smiled to herself hoping nobody in the salon had noticed, she'd felt almost fainting with excitement.

They'd danced until the end of the night, and she knew even at that early stage that Francis would be the love of her life.

There were tough times, saving what they could afford to get a place of their own, very tough times indeed but every moment wonderful because she had shared it with Francis.

Her nursing career was put on hold when the children came along. Mark, a beautiful boy, and Elizabeth, daddy's girl all the way.

All grown up now and making their own way in the world.

"How's that?" The young hairdresser sprayed her hair and gently removed the towel from her shoulders.

She slipped a little tip into her pocket as she affectionately held her coat for her at the cash desk. "Lizzie…there's no need for that…"

Walking home, she thought of how Francis would always put the money for her 'Hair do', as he'd call it, in the jar on the mantelpiece.

Every Friday without fail.

Goodness, where had the years gone!

Mark was a beautiful child, gentle and caring. Elizabeth on the other hand, was boisterous, would run rings around Mark. Only had eyes for her dad, and did he enjoy it. He'd never given one any more attention than the other of course but Elizabeth had him wrapped around her little fingers.

Now busy with children of their own, Lizzie would have liked to see a bit more of them but she understood all too well, between mortgages and childcare these days, sure they were like ships that pass in the night – working all hours to try to make ends meet.

Francis was sitting in his chair reading the paper when she got home. She knew the day was coming when she could no longer leave him on his own, but she wasn't going to think about that now, she would savour every moment of normality and deal with this one day at a time. "Cup of tea?" she'd nudged him as he drifted into sleep.

"Aw, there you are…Lizzie. Sure, I won't have you drinking on yer own…" He'd winked affectionately at her and added, "Maybe an old custard cream to go with it."

He was a devil for the sweet things.

Lizzie had noticed the change in Francis a while back, little things that only she would probably notice, she loved him so.

Elizabeth had a little girl, three now, called her after Francis. To his delight, she started to call her Franie then and it stuck.

She had her father's good looks, auburn hair and the darkest brown eyes ever seen. Her dad, Tim, was a gentleman, worked as a mechanic in the bus station. Worked all the hours he could to support his family.

Elizabeth though her own flesh and blood was hard work, Lizzie thought, wanted everything there and then. Liked to keep up with her friends though much better off than her. Had Franie in an expensive crèche when Lizzie herself would have been only too glad to take care of the little one when she returned to work.

It was seemingly good to let them mix with children of their own age. Lizzie never heard the like of it, not to mention, the cost!

Tim got on very well with Francis and Lizzie, often took Francis for a pint on a Sunday afternoon, didn't have to ask him twice, he'd have the jacket on as soon as Tim came through the door.

That was the first thing Lizzie had noticed, Francis struggling to get his hand into the sleeve of his coat. Could happen to anyone but this was different, the sleeve had come inside out last time he had worn it and he just couldn't make out what was wrong that he couldn't get his hand into it. Lizzie had helped him and made light of it and put it to the back of her mind. "Is Francis okay?" Tim came into the kitchen when they returned after a pint one Sunday, concern showing on his face. "…just, he seems sort of quiet…or something…not his usual chatty self…"

"Aw, sure he's probably fretting over something and nothing…you know how he frets…that'll be it…he's grand…" Lizzie too had noticed the quiet, or more kind of a distance in his presence lately. Sort of into himself, she knew if something was amiss, she would hear about it sooner or later. She had asked him when Tim had left that day if he had enjoyed his pint and he had answered as usual that he'd enjoyed the chat and how Tim was a lovely lad and always had time to give.

But which wasn't a bit like him, he had gone on to rant about Elizabeth, how she should come and visit her mother more and how she'd only had time for her so-called well-to-do friends.

It was so unlike Francis to talk about anyone in that manner let alone Elizabeth, the apple of his eye.

It was very much out of character for him, the anger in his voice.

Mark was their firstborn and Francis was ecstatic, the only boy in a houseful of women. H Emily, his mother, used to say, he was over the moon to have a son. Lizzie remembered how he used to take him on a little saddle on the crossbar of his bike on Saturdays, to watch the local football team play. No bicycle helmets in those days!

Mark was teased a lot in school as a child because he had a club foot and walked with a very slight limp. Lizzie recalled the visits to the clinics when he was only an infant for physiotherapy.

The screams of him as they tried to carry out the exercises, each time she struggled to hold back the tears.

Francis could not bear to go, it was enough to hear about it. He had worn braces up to his knee since the day he could walk. When he started school, the children used to laugh at him and call him names.

There were days she remembered that he would cry all the way home, not that he would ever admit it but the marks on his little face from his mucky hands after wiping away the tears were a real giveaway. He'd had one good buddy in school who'd always stand up for him, Freddie. It was Freddie who had spilt the beans one evening after school. He'd come over to have tea with Mark and do their homework. Lizzie was in the kitchen making pancakes for tea, Mark's favourite, when she heard the whispering, "What's all this whispering?" The boys hadn't realised she was so close and jumped with fright. "…Whispering in company is bad manners…didn't you ever hear that, Freddie? And you, Mark…I'm surprised at you too…"

Freddie went red as a berry and spurted it all out, how some of the older boys were making fun of Mark and making him cry but that he would always look out for him, "Always, I promise, Lizzie…always…"

Such a sweet child he was, children could be so cruel. Francis was very upset when she told him, but Mark was going to have to stand up to those bullies. It would do no good at all them going in to fight his battles for him, hard as it was to stand by and watch. Francis had said, "What doesn't kill you will make you stronger."

There were days when she could see he dreaded going to school.

There were days too that she had to bite her tongue in greeting the principle with the usual smile. *Things are so different now,* she thought. She wasn't sure which way was best, all she knew was that children could be very cruel, very cruel indeed.

Chapter 2

When Elizabeth was born, Mark was eight. They had wondered how he would take to having a sister after being the only child for so long, but they needn't have worried at all. He couldn't take his eyes off her. Francis had to go abroad with his job for six months shortly after Elizabeth was born, Army work.

Lizzie had been worried for the whole six months until he was home again.

She'd felt like she'd lost a limb without him. Theirs was such a close relationship from day one that she just couldn't bear to be without him.

Elizabeth had started to take notice by the time Francis returned from working abroad, she was now nine months old and as he picked her up out of her cot to say hello, she said her first word.

She had been gurgling and cooing for a while but nothing you could say was a word, then came, "Dada…"

It brought tears to his eyes. "My beautiful girl," he'd said while crying, looking on Lizzie and Mark who were starting to get a bit teary-eyed as well.

"Come here, you two. I have missed you all so much."

It had been a while since Freddie had called around when Mark told his mum that Freddie was going away. His mum and dad had decided to live apart and he would be going to live with his dad. Mark was so upset. "I will never have another friend like Freddie…" he had sobbed. "He was my best friend ever."

Lizzie held her little boy for as long as it took to reassure him that he would be okay and Freddie would be okay too.

She remembered her mother talking about a friend of hers who for some reason or other couldn't have children. Being the tough cookie her mother was, she had told her friend, "Sure it's God's will and if they don't make you laugh, they won't make you cry, girl." *So true!* Lizzie had cried along with him.

She too would miss Freddie.

Elizabeth had absolutely no interest in school, homework was a nightmare, a constant battle to get it done. Mark had done well in school but had decided to go for a trade rather than going on to college. Though Francis felt he would have done well in college, he didn't make his feelings known. He was old enough to know his own mind and sure as long as he was happy, wasn't that all that mattered?

After qualifying as a plumber, Mark got a job with the local council. A good steady job. Francis had said that he was so proud of him.

Not like Francis in looks but had many of his traits, Francis was such a kind soul, generous with his time and so very thoughtful.

Mark too could be like that. Kitty worked as a receptionist for the council, she would send the lads to their various jobs every day.

Mark had told his mum that he quite fancied asking her out but was afraid she might turn him down.

"Well, if you don't ask…you will never know. Will you?" Lizzie waved him off at the door and smiled.

Time goes by so fast, she thought to herself. Seemed only like a short time ago since she waved him off to school in his short pants and knee socks. She didn't have to ask how he got on, goodness, she didn't know how he'd gotten through the door with the width of the smile on his face, she was so happy for him. *That would be nearly ten years ago now,* she thought. *The twins, now eight and baby Eilish just gone a year.*

Elizabeth had left school without any qualifications and wanted to do a hairdressing course. Francis, so delighted to see her take an interest in something, agreed to fund it, and she could pay him back when she would start earning. "It's good to give her a bit of responsibility," he had said. Money, he would never see again!

She did a couple of months' training and got fed up with it, packed it in and lost her fees. Went working in the local shop and got fed up with that too, then started a little job in a bakery in the town.

Lizzie feared for her at times. She was a very popular girl growing up, always demanding money to go out with the girls. Francis was indeed a soft touch for her, he worried about her so, wouldn't sleep until she came home at night, would walk the floors if it was late. Tim had walked her home one night where she had gotten very drunk and troublesome in the pub. He'd recognised her from working in the area, said he'd often seen her walk past the bus station. Francis thanked him and he went off. "My dear girl…what are we to do with you at all…" he'd called for Lizzie and between them had got her up the stairs and into bed, clothes and all. They would have words the next day, not much point in talking to her tonight, they thought.

Elizabeth was feeling very sorry for herself the next morning, very sorry indeed. She too had noticed Tim working locally, she would pass by the bus station every day on the way to work at the bakery. Always moaned and said her talents were wasted there but seemed to be sticking to it well.

The proprietor was a friend of Francis and she was such a lovely lady, had put up with Elizabeth's bad timekeeping and moods for a long time now. Lizzie suspected if she hadn't been a friend of the family, she would be sacked long since.

She was mortified when she was told that Tim had brought her home the night before and the state she was in, mortified wasn't the word.

How would she even walk past the bus station again, let alone smile at him in passing like she did every morning. "Good morning…how are you feeling today?"

She had walked quickly past with her head down in the hope that she wouldn't be seen. She wished it would be raining and she could have put an umbrella up to hide behind. "Hi…" She would have to acknowledge his kindness in taking her home the night before, it would be rude not to. "Aww sure, don't mention it…wasn't a bother at all. Maybe we can go out sometime?"

They had the fastest roller coaster of a relationship Lizzie had ever witnessed, spent more time arguing than anything else. "That boy has the patience of a saint." Lizzie had answered the door to Tim only to tell him Elizabeth had decided to go out with her friends at the last minute. Even though he'd made arrangements the previous night to take her out. "The patience of a saint…"

Francis would say nothing.

When she announced that they were getting married, Elizabeth had surprised them, Lizzie quietly wondered if there was an ulterior motive, *surely not!*

She hadn't been far wrong, Franie was born not six months after the big lavish wedding with all the trimmings, Tim took her on a cruise for their honeymoon. She would have everything she asked for when she asked for it or there would be a row.

She had joined a fancy gym and got in with a group of girls whose husbands could well afford their memberships unlike Tim. She was living way beyond their means and continued to do so.

Franie was a lovely child, loved to go to feed the ducks with Francis. He was so tall walking beside her and she was so tiny, it made him look even taller, he doted on her.

Francis got up to take the cups to the sink as he always did, a quick peck on the cheek as he passed her by, as he always did.

They would have laughed in the past when he would touch her every time he'd pass her by in the kitchen, she'd be preparing dinner or washing the pots. "One of these days you'll do that…and somebody will be watching," she used to say and they'd laugh and he'd hug her even tighter. She was already beginning to miss the old Francis, she watched as he stopped for a moment at the sink as if he'd forgotten in that short period of time what he was about to do.

The doorbell rang and as she hurried down the hall to open it, she could see the familiar silhouette through the glass. It was Jeffrey from next door, coming to take his old friend for a drive. "Hi, Lizzie, thought I might go for a little drive...wondered if Francis might like to join me, save me talking to the steering wheel."

Jeffrey was such a kind soul, he squeezed Lizzie's hand as he walked past her in the hallway. He was going out of his way to take his friend out and it wasn't the first time. He too could see the change in Francis. Lizzie remembered when he was first diagnosed, a few years since now, Jeffrey was the first outside of the family she'd told.

He wouldn't be one to feed the curious, of which there were many in these parts, no, he would have felt her pain as much as one of the family.

Jeffrey had lost his wife a couple of years after they had married.

Lizzie had never met Barbara but almost seemed like she knew her all her life, he'd talked so much about her. She always wished she had known her.

He was a gardener by profession, his was the most beautiful garden on the street. Seemed to have colours all the year round. Every morning, hail, rain or snow, you could see Jeffrey tending to his pots. Lizzie liked to potter around in the garden too but it had been neglected for too long. Somehow, she hadn't had the heart.

When they first moved into the house, Mark was just a baby, she remembered Francis working every evening after coming in from his work to put a swing in the garden. Got some rope from the lads on the boats down the docks and then made a timber seat. He'd made a good job of it too, that swing caused so many tantrums with Elizabeth, Lizzie recalled. She would be playing away with her dolls in the garden, happy as

Larry, never wanting to use the swing until Mark would come along to use it, then she'd want to be on it too, and there'd be a tantrum. Now, as she looked out of the window into the garden, the swing was just a reminder of those happy times, though at the time it seemed like the days were filled with work and hardship, but looking back now they were the happiest days of her life, if only she could have that time all over again.

It was Sunday, a beautiful spring day. Lizzie had asked Mark, Kitty and the children over for lunch, she had asked Elizabeth and Tim too and Franie of course, but Elizabeth had other plans. She would call by during the week, maybe Franie could go to feed the ducks with her Poppy.

Lizzie just smiled, she knew her daughter only too well, she would be dining out, somewhere posh no doubt. She doubted Tim would even hear about the invitation.

A nice leg of lamb with roast potatoes, carrot and parsnip and gravy, that should do nicely, she'd thought. Francis would never complain, you could put anything up to him and he'd eat it. Always thanked her afterwards and said, "That was lovely," not a scrap left on the plate.

Chapter 3

Mark handed her a box of sweets. “You shouldn’t have.”

He smiled and kissed the top of her head. “Thanks for this, Mam.”

“Sure, you’re welcome anytime, you know that.”

Lizzie would have loved to have felt as close to Elizabeth as she felt with Mark, but that closeness was never there, not for the want of trying. Many a tear she had shed when her efforts had been thrown back in her face. At times, made almost to feel a nuisance, a bother for her to answer a question to. Growing up, she had been spoiled.

Lizzie remembered sometimes having to give in to her in the shop to avoid a tantrum in front of everyone.

“You’ll regret that.” An old lady was looking on.

No truer words had ever been spoken. Elizabeth knew when to turn on the tears and if that didn’t work, you could expect a tantrum. She would be sent to her room only to find she had climbed out of the window. Lizzie remembered one time when Francis had sent her to her room for being cheeky and demanding, now he would give in to her a hundred times a day but if he caught her being cheeky or answering her mother back, which she’d done on a regular basis, he would send her to her room.

She didn't like it when Francis got cross with her, she would bang the doors as she went and pound her way up the stairs.

There had been a knock on the door. Francis still a bit quiet for having to send Elizabeth to her room, it would upset him more than it would do Elizabeth, had gone out to answer it.

There, standing as bold as brass was Elizabeth and Alice from a few doors down. "Was just coming out of Jeffrey's there and noticed this lady sliding down the pipe from the window. Goodness, she could have broken her neck. What…" Turning to Elizabeth she'd continued, "Broken your neck, young lady." Turning on her heel, she took off down the path, Francis had shouted after her to thank her but she'd just given him a look of disgust.

There had been rumours that Alice had a soft spot for Jeffrey for a long time now, was often seen bringing him some of her home cooking or walking back from mass together on a Sunday.

Aw sure, Elizabeth was a nightmare!

"That was delicious…as usual." Mark took his plate to the sink.

"Plenty more in the oven if you want it." Lizzie always cooked for an army, Francis would say. "Thanks Mam, stuffed," and off he went into the sitting room to join Francis who'd already settled into his afternoon nap. More than likely, Mark wouldn't be far behind him.

It was nice to have the bit of company, the children playing outside, a nice cup of tea and a natter with Kitty. She'd asked about Elizabeth. Kitty had given up her job when the children came along.

Mark had left it up to herself to decide, gave her the option of staying at home or organising a crèche for them. He'd said that he would be happy either way, he had a good steady job and could afford to give her the choice. Lizzie had offered to take the twins if she decided to return to work but while she had appreciated the offer, she wanted to stay at home and look after them herself. "I don't want to miss a moment," she had said.

Sitting down to a nice cup of tea, Lizzie had let out a big sigh. "Lizzie, I hope you don't mind me saying, but you're looking a bit tired. You really didn't have to do lunch for us today, you have enough to be doing."

Kitty was so caring and thoughtful, better than a daughter to her, she thought. "I'm grand; it's lovely to have you all around."

"…believe Elizabeth is into the keep fit these days, Tim was telling Mark, met him in O'Malley's the other evening."

"Goodness, it was nine o clock, I'd forgotten to get cereal and you know Seanie where cereal is concerned. Sure he'd live on it, all hell would break loose if he got up in the morning and there was no cereal. He said he was working late, appreciated the overtime, said those classes don't come cheap."

Lizzie couldn't help but feel resentment for her daughter, not that she wanted to, in fact quite the opposite, she wanted to see the caring thoughtful side of her but there wasn't any of that to be seen.

Elizabeth only ever thought of Elizabeth and that was the truth of it, she loved her all the same and longed to be a part of her life, each day proving to be less and less so. Francis, through no fault of his own, was now becoming more dependent on Lizzie by the day, and Elizabeth though so close to her dad growing up, now seemed uninterested, even ashamed of him.

It had been hard to get him to shave or wash these days, Lizzie would have to remind him to change his clothes. Elizabeth, when she did take time to fit them in, would spend her short visit dictating to her mother, "Can't you get him to shave? He looks like he's slept in his clothes…there's a smell Mam…don't you get it…what if other people notice…"

She'd never offer to help or notice that Lizzie was exhausted with taking care of him as best she could, not good enough apparently, in Elizabeth's opinion. Her heart was breaking a little bit more every day as she watched the love of her life be consumed by this dreadful illness. She was doing her best.

Francis had slept for an hour after Mark, Kitty and the children had gone. "Let him sleep," Mark had said. "Looks comfortable…tell him I'll call round tomorrow, have a chat."

Lizzie had washed the last pot and turned to hang her apron on the handle of the door as she always did, Francis had been standing behind her and she hadn't noticed.

"How long have you been standing there?" She noticed a tear in his eye. "You okay, Francis…are you ill? Come, sit down." She took him by the hand, his hands were so cold though the kitchen was warm

He seemed to shuffle along the floor, Lizzie looked to see if maybe his shoes were untied and loose but he wasn't wearing them, he had taken them off in the sitting room before he had his nap.

"What is it, Francis, why are you crying?" She struggled to hold back the tears herself, he looked so lost and sad.

"Francis…" She put her arms around him and let him cry until he looked at her lovingly and took her hands in his.

"My prayers, Lizzie, I can't remember my prayers…"

There was a frightened look in his eyes she would never forget.

Francis would say his prayers every morning without fail, when the children were young, he would kneel with them at bedtime beside their beds and give thanks for the day, often checking Elizabeth for giggling into her hands. His faith was very important to him.

The day had been so lovely with Mark, Kitty and the children round for lunch, for a short while it was as if everything was normal.

Lizzie got the feeling though that all was not rosy, Mark was out of sorts, something just wasn't right, maybe she was imagining things.

Elizabeth hadn't called in the week as she said she would, Lizzie wondered why this was so surprising to her. Wasn't the first time she'd let them down after all. Just with it being Mother's Day, she thought she might.

Mark had dropped in with the twins all right, Kitty had sent her best wishes. "Sit down and have a cup of tea."

Lizzie put the flowers the twins had handed her into a vase and filled the kettle.

Sure they had half of them broken, pulling them from one to the other wanting to be the one to hand them to nanny.

Seanie was the competitive one, always wanting to be ahead of Alfie, would race to get to the door first, race to ring the bell and nearly knock you over in trying to be the first to give you a hug. Alfie was sort of gentle in his ways, always standing back to let Seanie have his way.

Both so different even in looks, you would never take them for brothers not to mind twins. Francis loved to see the boys coming, there would have been a fight back in the day when they were toddlers to sit on Poppy's knee, he would take out his shiny medals from his early days in the army and watch the excitement on their little faces.

"I'm going to be a soldier like Poppy when I get big," Seanie would often say. Alfie would echo, "Me too."

"Mam..." Mark had left the boys in the sitting room and put the TV on for them. "...I was talking to Tim." Mark got up to close the kitchen door before he continued, "It's Elizabeth. Tim is having an awful time with her, he thinks she's seeing someone...another man."

Lizzie didn't know what to say. She knew when he'd come round for dinner that day that Mark had something on his mind. She just knew there was something.

Next day, Francis was gone with Jeffrey next door for a drive around, he'd sat to have a bit of lunch with them after. Lizzie was delighted, a bit of company for Francis. Maybe he would eat a bit with Jeffrey eating a bit. Didn't seem to have much of an appetite these days. Lizzie had noticed he'd lost a bit of weight too. Not that he was ever overweight, always trim but well-built, he would have turned a head or two in uniform back in the day.

How would he deal with Elizabeth being unfaithful to her husband? Why hadn't she come round and told them herself? Was she ashamed? Did she even know the meaning of the word?

Poor Tim, he was such a nice fellow and so good to her. Goodness, she never wanted for anything. Mark had said he was out of his mind with worry, and Franie, where did she fit into her mother's newfound friendship. It was a mess. Lizzie would ring her and ask her to call round.

"Hi pops…how are you doing old man?" Elizabeth held a bunch of flowers in her hand as she came through the door full of the joy.

"Sorry, I didn't get here for Mother's Day; better late than never, eh." She handed the flowers to Lizzie and went to the fridge.

"Starving. Anything nice?"

Lizzie made some tea and put some fresh scones that she had baked in the morning on a plate.

"How are you? Haven't seen you in a while."

Lizzie looked up as she buttered a scone for Francis, he loved the home baking.

"God bless ya." He would catch her hand as she walked away.

"You two…like young love birds." Elizabeth looked on as she put jam on her scone, never lost her sweet tooth. Didn't have to worry about her figure; she was a beauty by nature. Pity it only seemed to be skin deep.

Lizzie felt bitter towards her.

"How's Tim?" Lizzie wasn't sure if that was an appropriate question with what Mark had told her, but she had just automatically asked like she always would. Elizabeth hadn't said anything to them about any bother until then.

Chapter 4

“Boring as usual.” She hadn’t even looked up from buttering her second scone. “Only so much boredom you can take…plenty more fish in the sea.” Francis seemed oblivious to the conversation going on in the room and Lizzie for once was grateful. Marriage was for lifetime as far as he was concerned, wouldn’t hear of it any other way.

She remembered, once coming home from doing the shopping having been shocked herself on hearing that Maisie, her lifelong friend, had decided to leave her Harry. He’d been drinking and carrying on and she was sick of it, when she’d told Francis, he’d just looked over his reading glasses disgusted.

“Don’t be talking like that now, Lizzie, it isn’t right,” and dismissed her.

“Elizabeth, what about your vows…Franie…your beautiful house…wake up and look around you. You has the best husband in the world. He must be heartbroken…you can’t do that to him…think on now, young lady.”

Lizzie might as well be talking to the teapot and she knew it, Elizabeth would do whatever Elizabeth wanted to do. To hell with the consequences, it went in one ear and out the other.

She thought maybe while she was there with her dad, she would ask her to sit with him for a little while and Lizzie could run to the shop, do her good to spend some time with him, it had been a while. There was shouting as she walked up the pathway on her return, in her rush to get the key in the door, she dropped it. Francis was holding Elizabeth by her wrists when she got in and shouting out,

"Leave it. Leave it…"

Elizabeth looked round as the door opened.

"Mam, thank God you're back. I was only going to give him a shave. He pulled my hand and the blade slipped and caught him. When I went to get a tissue to wipe the blood away, he started shouting at me…caught me by the wrists."

There was a shiver in her voice as she started to cry.

"Okay Francis…it's okay…" Lizzie gently released his grip from Elizabeth and held his hands for a minute. "It's okay, my love…everything's okay…"

Francis had that same look in his eyes she had seen the day he told her he couldn't remember his prayers. It was like there was no light in them, just a vague look, a vacant stare; it was awful.

She would let him settle a bit and then clean his face. It was only a tiny cut, he wasn't going to bleed to death, might only aggravate him more to clean it now. She felt for Elizabeth, it can't have been easy looking at her dad like that, the one she'd looked up to, ran to when she was in trouble or needed a few bobs to go out with her friends. The one that had never let her down, now barely recognisable in his ways, aggressive and angry, traits never accustomed to with the dad she grew up with.

Not wanting her mam to see her cry and let down her guard, Elizabeth got her jacket and was gone out of the door before Lizzie had a chance to talk to her. Maybe she wasn't as tough as she came across to most people as being, maybe there was a heart that felt emotion ticking in there, but why was she so cold?

Francis had settled a bit when Lizzie came back into the kitchen, having shouted after Elizabeth and been ignored. She put the kettle on and brought him a cup of tea, the blood had dried on his chin so she left him to enjoy his tea and biscuits. Standing with her back to him at the sink pretending to be busy, she welled up with tears, her heart ached. She needed Francis to be Francis, she was nothing without his support. This was so hard.

The phone rang, it was early morning. Lizzie half afraid to answer it in case it was bad news, lifted the receiver with a shaking hand.

"Lizzie…I'm so sorry to call so early." It was Tim.

"It's Franie, I think she's running a temperature. I don't know what to do. Elizabeth didn't come home last night, what should I do? She's crying for her mum." Tim was frantic.

Turned out Franie was teething. Tim, under the instructions of Lizzie, took her to the doctor who made the diagnosis very quickly.

Her mum was nowhere to be found; he didn't like leaving her with Lizzie but she insisted. He'd had a job to go to after all, someone had to provide. Lizzie was only too happy to help.

When Elizabeth turned up at the door, still under the influence of drink from the night before, Lizzie wanted to give her a piece of her mind. What was she thinking? Out all night and a baby at home, not to mention a husband. But there was no use in talking to her then, she had stretched on the couch after mumbling that Tim had left a note to say where Franie was, and she was asleep in no time.

Goodness what a mess!

Franie was having a bad day, sobbed and sobbed, Lizzie had her on her lap trying to get her to sleep for a while but when she'd heard her mum speak, she was up like a shot. She stood looking at her mum sleeping on the couch, her dummy in her mouth and her face wet with tears. Elizabeth was out for the count.

Franie huddled up beside her and sobbed away until she finally went to sleep too.

The evenings were getting longer as the summer crept in, Lizzie loved the brightness of the summer evenings. *Would do your heart good,* she'd thought. Jeffrey had come over to tidy up the garden, asked of course first if Lizzie would like him to do it. Had a few plants over if she wanted him to do a few pots for her, he was such a sweetheart.

Maybe Francis could help, he'd said, the fresh air would do him the world of good and Lizzie could get on with her pottering around.

Sometimes, friends could be better than family, Lizzie thought.

She'd watched as Francis walked along after Jeffrey in the garden (shuffling along) and how Jeffrey had asked his opinion as to where to plant. Arms folded as if supervising the work. *They are laughing and having a good old time,* she thought.

Mark then arrived with the boys, delighted to see his dad out in the garden, he walked over and gave him a pat on the back.

"Hard at it." Seanie and Alfie were making a Beeline for the door. *Or more the biscuit jar,* Lizzie thought as she smiled, it was so lovely to see them.

"Hi, Mam. Lovely to see Dad doing a bit…"

Kettle on the boil, she called the men in for a cup of tea. Francis looked tired, seemed to tire easily these days.

Jeffrey pulled the chair out from the table

"Sit yourself down there, young man…thinks we have enough done for one day." He winked at Lizzie.

She would always put the milk and sugar in the tea for him, even before he'd gotten ill. A couple of biscuits to dunk and he was happy. These days, she could only leave two biscuits on the plate beside him or he would eat the whole plate of them.

While dunking his biscuit, he accidently toppled the cup and spilled the tea all over the table.

"No harm…no harm." Lizzie would have to be quick before he got upset by it. Especially with the children around, she didn't want them seeing him upset.

All cleaned up, she gave him a fresh cup of tea and a couple of biscuits. As Mark looked on, he could see things were getting more difficult by the day for his mam. He'd discussed a nursing home, maybe to give her a break but Lizzie wouldn't hear of it.

"You know, Mam, the day might come when Dad will need twenty-four-hour care." Lizzie knew only too well how hard things could and probably would get but she was going to look after Francis as long as she had an ounce of energy left in her body. As she left the second lot of biscuits on the plate beside him, Francis took her hand in his now so frail hand, with a dribble of tea on his chin he smiled at her and said,

"Are you my wife?" She loved him so much. Her heart was breaking as she kissed his forehead and wiped his chin, *Nothing will part them.*

Lizzie had left home when she was eighteen. Badly treated by her dad, she had little confidence in herself, had moved in with her school mate, Maisie, both taking waitressing jobs to put themselves through college.

She'd always wanted to do nursing. Herself and Maisie had planned it since they'd started secondary school. Once they were able to pay their rent and have a couple of nights out in the week, sure wouldn't they be away with it. No more terrifying nights waiting for her dad to come home drunk and rowing with her mother until all hours, shouting abuse at her and her sister in the morning, suffering from a hangover. Never physically abusive thankfully but both bore the scars of the mental abuse they had suffered.

Her sister, Margaret, wasn't as ambitious as her, waited at home only to be abused more as she got older. After the death of her mother, she had stayed on to look after the man that had made her life a misery until his body finally gave in to the curse of drink. Margaret started to drink herself then at home, a secret drinker, the worst kind. Lizzie had tried many times to get her to come and stay with her for a little break, or to meet up for a chat but she was never interested. At the age of fifty-two, she was found dead, reported to have choked on her own vomit.

The home house now practically in ruins from neglect would be Lizzie's to do what she wanted to do with it. She'd had no interest in it whatsoever, she had worked hard along with Francis to get a home of their own by then, had paid off the mortgage and her family had grown. She remembered thinking if only she'd had the option of selling a property in the days when things were so tough, when they'd struggled to make ends meet. But it doesn't work like that!

It was years before she had the courage to go round there, even then, the memories had come flooding back; the shouting, the smell of drink, the cold feeling of the room on the day her sister lay in a heap after choking on her vomit. All came flooding back. Best to be rid of the place, she had decided, there was nothing happy about this place.

She let it go for a song, couldn't justify asking the market value for a property that was falling down around her ears, probably needed to be knocked.

Some said she should have gotten more for it but she had taken the first offer and wished the young couple luck with it.

If life had taught her one thing, it was that money wasn't everything, lots more precious things in life.

Elizabeth and Tim seemed to be pulling together again. Francis was delighted to see them call with Franie. She would hand him her dummy and climb up on his knee and then take it back from him again.

Lizzie had spent the morning sprucing him up. Got him in the shower, changed his clothes and even got him to shave. She had bought him an electric shaver and he seemed to manage it much better than the wet shave. Missed the odd bit but sure that was okay, he was doing his best.

"You're looking good, Francis." Tim sat in the chair beside him, keeping an eye on Franie at the same time. She was up to all sorts of mischief these days and was doing her best to take off her Poppy's glasses. She always called him Poppy, no one ever knew where that came from. Not succeeding to take the glasses off, she went on to fiddle with his ear with her thumb in her mouth, dummy left aside.

Chapter 5

Lizzie made her way into the kitchen to make a cup of tea, Elizabeth followed her in, "Mam, I-I'm sorry for being such a pain in…"

There were tears in her eyes.

"What brought this on?" Lizzie wanted to lighten the moment.

"Just…I know it's not easy. I should be of more help…not…not so selfish."

She was like a little child that had done something wrong and came back to say she was sorry, not the Elizabeth Lizzie knew, not at all.

"Here, make yourself useful and take in the tea." She handed her the tray and gave her a puzzled look, she was puzzled, something was going on.

Elizabeth left the tray down on the worktop and turned to face Lizzie,

"I'm pregnant, Mam…"

"Isn't that great news?" Lizzie wanted to hug her daughter but she pulled away.

"It's not Tim's. We…we've not been together in that way for a long time. I'm so ashamed. I don't know what to do. I don't know who the father is, I don't remember." She came to Lizzie and cried her fill.

At last, her daughter had come to her but the circumstances were the last thing Lizzie would have wished for.

It seems when she discovered she was pregnant and couldn't remember who she'd been with, it had frightened her, frightened her so much that she had taken a good look at her life. Her drinking, her selfishness, her family and how she had ignored the advice offered by her mother. She had been nothing but a selfish spoiled biddy who didn't deserve her wonderful husband, her beautiful daughter and a family who cared so much.

"It's too little too late, I know. I will have lost him by now…he's put up with me for so long…you all have…it's a mess, Mam…an awful mess."

Being a mother to a child is the very same as being a mother to an adult, same unconditional love, same trust and same heartache.

Lizzie would support her daughter through thick and thin, she may very well come along the next week and be her old selfish self again but we live in the moment of now, now is all that matters. Seems when you have found true love, unconditional love in your partner in life, the same applies. After her breaking his heart in breaking the news to Tim, it took a bit of time but he accepted her for what she was and loved her the whole way through it. Joe's arrival in the early hours of the morning on Christmas day brought joy beyond words. Whether it was the hormones or just the reality of it all, it had changed Elizabeth, she appreciated things now, she lived for her little family.

She, too, now realised that Tim could have turned his back on her but he didn't, though broken, he'd picked up the pieces and kept going. A wonderful dad to Franie and now looked like being a wonderful dad to Joe.

Mark had hurt his back and was out of work, was lost not being able to drive or help out with the children. Had to walk miles every day for the exercise, called in most mornings for a chat or to pass the time.

Lizzie felt for him, although being paid while out of work, he just wasn't one to be hanging around, it was killing him. He would buy the paper and read it along with Francis, "Awful news Dad, isn't it?" He'd read about a storm on the east coast that had left families without homes and was a proper disaster. Francis was looking at him and smiling.

Mark looked at Lizzie. "I don't know if he knows me today…seems a bit distant…"

Turning back to his dad he asked, "Who am I? Do you know who I am?"

Smiling as ever, Francis nodded his head and replied, "I know, I love you…" Mark got up to take his cup to the sink and kissed his mother on the top of her head. Returning to the table, he put his hand on top of hers that already cupped his dad's hand and off he went.

Lizzie didn't know whether she had gotten harder with the years or just plain used to the sadness of it all. Or maybe she had cried enough.

It had rained for weeks on end. Finally, there was a lovely sunny dry day, perfect to hang out the wash. There was plenty of washing these days. Getting less aware, Francis seldom made it to the toilet on time now and the bedclothes had to be changed most days. Lizzie remembered a time when she'd wanted Francis to move the single bed from their room to make more space. They always had a double and a single in the room since the children were small, came in handy at night when one of them couldn't sleep and wanted to cuddle up with their mam. Francis would go into the single bed. Nowadays, she was so glad they never got to move it.

Lizzie would never be able to have Francis in another room, it was hard enough having to have him in another bed but that was necessary now. She would lie awake most nights watching him in case she didn't hear him call, watching, wondering and wishing things could be like they were before. It was like there was a dense fog and he was disappearing in it, she was losing sight of him.

"Goodness, it's a windy one." She'd come in out of the backyard after hanging out the wash, delighted with herself.

"Can't beat the fresh smell off the clothes when you dry them outside." Looking around the door into the kitchen, Francis seemed slouched forward on his chair. Doctor on the way, she held him close.

"Not today…please God…not today…I'm not ready."

After a full examination, it was realised Francis had a chest infection.

"Knocks a lot out of a patient with other issues going on…will have knocked him back quite a bit. Lizzie, I know your feelings about putting him into care…but what about a few days of respite." Knowing the answer would be no, the doctor proceeded to write a prescription and handed it to Mark who had arrived as fast as he could. Elizabeth had left Joe with a neighbour, fearing the worst. Hopeless in a crisis, she had fallen to pieces on the way. Franie ran to sit on Poppy's lap but Mark caught her before she reached him.

"Poppy is feeling a little bit bad today…maybe we'll sit here." And he sat on a chair beside him, taking Franie on his lap.

"Poppy wants my dummy? Make him all better." Franie took her dummy out of her mouth and tried to put it into her poppy's mouth.

At times, Franie would remind Lizzie of Elizabeth when she was her age, up to all sorts. She was reminded of a time when Francis would come in from work and as usual, reach out to hug her. If Elizabeth was in the room, she would whinge and push her way between them to get her dad's attention. Once up in his arms, she was happy again. Often, he would take Lizzie's arm just to tease Elizabeth and would hug them both. "Let's have a big family hug." He'd wink at Lizzie, knowing what her reaction would be.

"No, Daddy…just Elizabeth…no Mummy…" But they'd hug anyway.

Franie was quiet as a mouse, one would think she knew something was going on, she'd sat without a move, watching her poppy.

Once the antibiotics had kicked in, Francis was back to his old self again. Well, the most recent self. With no choice but to get used to it, Lizzie was grateful for that itself. Mark had returned to work after his back trouble. Though told by his doctor that his job wasn't helping his condition and to consider a less strenuous job. That went in one ear and out the other.

There would be a mass on Sunday and a reception after for deceased members of the army took place every year around the same time.

Francis would insist Lizzie get a new dress for the occasion, there would be the most beautiful food, often three or four courses and a band would play in the hall after. Sure you wouldn't be able to dance after all you would be eating, but they did. They danced and danced, it was like there was no one else in the room when they danced, looking into each other's eyes so close, you wouldn't get a rib of hair between them. It was a memory that would stay with her for the rest of her years. She wasn't sure he would be up to it this year.

Fr Waters, the parish priest of the area had called for his usual visit.

"I have arranged for yourself and Francis to be picked up for the army reception, don't know why they invite me every year but sure…isn't that the way…sure it'll be a night out for us."

Lizzie didn't want to offend the man but she wasn't at all sure Francis would enjoy it. "Father, I think maybe we might give it a miss this year…you know…I mean I don't know if Francis would enjoy it."

"Don't be daft woman…sure he'll have a ball…do you good too, to get out for a night…meet all his friends…sure he'll be grand…eh!"

Though a bit apprehensive, Lizzie was glad she had gone. They skipped the mass, just went for dinner and stayed for a bit of the music and dancing. She ironed his old army suit and pinned on his medals. Shining as usual, he would often take them out of the drawer and shine them.

With him sitting on the bed, she laced up his army boots, she hadn't noticed before how thin his legs must have got, tying them as tight as she could, his feet were still swimming in them. She'd put on an extra pair of socks to make them fit better. It was heart-wrenching to see him look so frail in his uniform, once a fine build of a man.

Some came up to chat to him at the dinner, bursting out of their uniform with middle age spread, some too upset to stop and speak, just a shake of the hands. He was enjoying it though, she thought, though there would be no dancing this time. She watched as the couples waltzed across the floor and she took his hand in hers, it felt so cold. As she looked across at Francis, there was a tear rolling down his face, still managing a smile he nodded as if he too was remembering days gone by? "Great night, Francis eh…" Fr Waters was in great demand for the waltzing, the sweat was pouring out of him.

"…sure they have me half killed…I'm not able for all that twisting and turning and I half crippled…it's an effort to get up on the altar these days…stop."

Evening time was always Lizzie's favourite time of the day, children washed and fed and tucked up in bed, herself and Francis sitting side by side on the couch, often holding hands, more often snoozing, but always comfortable in each other's company. He would talk about the day, fill in the hours they were apart, she would talk about the children, little things that might have happened in his absence, that he might have missed out on.

Maybe Mark playing a match at school, or Elizabeth might have lost a tooth, ordinary everyday things. She could never remember going to bed on a night without him saying, "I love you," and she would answer,

"I love you more."

It had been a long time since Lizzie had heard Mark speak of his old school mate Freddie, had sort of lost touch along the way.

"Can't imagine Freddie joining the priesthood...it's hilarious..."

Mark was laughing as he spoke about his chat with Fr Watters the day before, "...and we have a local boy now joining the priesthood..."

He couldn't believe his ears, Freddie!

Chapter 6

Lizzie reminded him that all those years ago, Freddie was the one true friend he'd had at school and always came across as a very caring young lad. "Ya, but the priesthood…" Mark sat reminiscing for a while, he seemed to remember every act of bullying that went on and how Freddie would stand up to them. "I distinctly remember this one guy," he'd said, "…was much older than us, followed us round the corner out of sight of the school…cute enough…he knew we wouldn't dream of reporting him the next day or he'd do worse. He had us well warned…he'd heard Freddie had a birthday the day before and reckoned he'd have some birthday money…he took every penny of it, Mam. Freddie intended going to the shop to treat us both out of his money…" Lizzie listened intently.

What a bully, she'd thought.

"Not sorry that part of my life is over…don't think that sort of thing goes on in schools nowadays…but who knows…could be some young lad dreading getting up in the morning as much as I did."

"It's a feeling you never forget; almost feel sick to my stomach even thinking about it."

A lot of water under the bridge since then.

Francis would have talked to Mark every day about bullies and how they were cowards behind it all.

"Always went around in groups, wouldn't be half so smart if you met one of them on their own. Best avoided, best to walk away and ignore their remarks, nothing annoys their sort as much as being ignored. Be the bigger man and walk away." She would always remember his words. Sometimes easier said than done though.

Emily, Francis's mum, had told Lizzie how she'd had a path worn up and down to the school where Francis would come home with his jumper torn or his books scribbled on. One time, she remembered he'd run away from home because of a gang of youngsters who threatened to throw him into the well down the road if he didn't do their homework for them, seems the principal's son was the ringleader. It was awful going on. She'd said, "I didn't care whose son he was…I went right up to him and told him everything that was going on…wasn't long changing his tune." Francis was a shy sort, didn't like his mother going to the school, she said but children can't be getting away with that.

Back when Mark was being bullied at school, Lizzie had wondered why Francis had insisted on Mark standing up for himself, maybe it put him in mind of his own experience but he'd never mentioned it, nor had she. His mother had told her in confidence, that's the way it would stay, a lovely lady, his mother a real motherly way about her, cried for days seemingly when Francis decided to follow his father's footsteps and join the army. Once over the shock, there was no one as proud as she was of him. With three daughters and Francis the only boy, sure he was spoiled rotten. "But always had manners, mind…taught all of our children respect…very important…won't go far wrong in the world if you have respect," she had said.

Dee (or Deirdre) Francis's oldest sister, married a farmer and had settled very well into country life, loved it and would never live in the city again, she'd said. Came to visit on the odd occasion. She did come into town, a little late in life getting married, they didn't have any children of their own. She used to love to spoil Mark and Elizabeth when they were babies, buying outfits for them every time she called, nothing cheap either. Lizzie would get on to her and she would laugh.

"Sure, who else can I spend it on…there's no tow bar on the hearse."

Lizzie loved her company and always had a story, no harm in her at all but she would take off in a rant and leave you gobsmacked.

Her husband, Bartley, would put up with awful abuse altogether, Francis would often say after she'd left, "We know who wears the pants in that house…" and they would have a laugh. She was harmless, had a big heart.

Sarah and Josephine were twins, Francis always thought maybe that was where Marks twins came in, had skipped a generation.

Two very different personalities altogether, Sarah was a bit posh, full of her own importance and was infuriated with her sister's lack of elegance. Lizzie remembered the day herself and Francis got married. With Maisie as her bridesmaid, Francis had asked Sarah's husband Eric or Smokey, as he was called in his army days, to be his best man: they being old army mates and all.

Sarah had nearly outshone the bride turning up in a beautiful off-white costume, with beaded pearls around her neck, all that was missing was the veil. It didn't matter to Lizzie though. On the day, nothing was going to put a shadow on her heart of sunshine. Josephine, on the other hand, had worn a grey overcoat with a burnt orange hat and blue boots.

"Wouldn't you think you'd make an effort?" Sarah gave her sister a look of disapproval, Josephine just shrugged her shoulders as if confused by her sister's remark.

Francis had smiled at Lizzie, she remembered

"Nobody deserves to be this happy…" he'd said and he kissed her.

Francis often spoke about Eric, how he kept their spirits up when they'd be missing home if they were on duty abroad. He'd always lighten the moment with a funny story or two, always up to no good. And a devil for the cigarettes. Would give away his food vouchers for a cigarette, he was addicted. Hence the nickname Smokey.

Eric and Sarah were so different, they used to say opposites attract when they'd be in their company. Always went to the army do's together. Francis and herself and Sarah and Eric.

Eric would have the place covered in smoke before the night was over, Sarah would throw him one of her disgusted looks and in the grandest of accents, "Darling, I do wish you would leave us some air to breathe…before you contaminate the place with your tobacco smoke…" And the silk handkerchief would be taken out of the purse to fan away the smoke. Often she would proceed to move her chair ever so slightly away from the flow of smoke without bringing attention to herself of course. They were after all in the midst of dignitaries and heroes, aged and crippled from years gone by but nevertheless heroes.

Wonderful memories.

Josephine had never married, finished her degree in college and took off to see the world. Francis was very close to Josephine, he'd got on well with all three but always spoke of Josephine with a glint in his eye. He once told Lizzie how he'd climbed a tree in the back garden to rescue her where she had read a story about a girl who had climbed the highest tree and discovered if the wind was blowing in the right direction she could fly. Ever the adventurer, she would have to try it, only to discover when she got to the top, she couldn't even look down let alone fly, she had screamed her head off.

It had taken him the best part of the afternoon to get her down, trying not to look down she had closed her eyes.

"How can you see where you're going if you don't open your eyes…" Francis was standing on the nearest branch, unable to reach her unless she stepped forward.

"I can't…I'll fall…I can't." Eventually he'd talked her into sitting on her bottom and sliding her way down to him, she'd done it with her eyes still closed.

"She was like a baby kangaroo, holding on for dear life…" he'd smiled. "That was the end of her adventures into flying." She could only have been about four or five years old.

He'd wondered if she still remembered it. Lizzie, now wondered if Francis still remembered it, he seemed to talk about years ago yet the previous day's events were difficult for him to recall these days. What a cruel disease this was, what a waste of a beautiful mind.

Francis's father, Owen was an army man, true and true, very regimental in every aspect of life seemingly, quite strict as a father, Francis would say but fair at the same time. He'd often spoke of his fishing trips with him as a youngster, he loved to fish, they'd had many a chat man to man on those fishing trips.

"Always be a man of your word Francis…your character is worth its weight in gold…you lose that…you lose everything…and be honest with yourself…" He'd told him wise words. He was so proud of his dad, he'd watch him pin his medals onto his jacket with eyes as big as oranges, his mother would say.

Owen too had been a victim to Alzheimer's disease, indeed Lizzie truly believed it was hereditary although not proven, almost the same age to the day when Francis had been struck down with the dreadful torment that is Alzheimer's.

Elizabeth had done some research into her dad's condition when he'd been diagnosed, only now Lizzie had discovered that for a long time she had battled with the fear of developing it herself. Perhaps, explaining the anger she had shown in the early days, and her absence from her father's side at times when she was most needed. The fear of seeing her own destiny in her father's eyes, Lizzie had no idea that she had been going through such tough times.

It was no excuse for her drinking and carrying on, but she'd said she'd tried to block it out, she was being eaten up with fear. Seems, she had discussed it with Mark, asked if he'd ever worried about it. Mark had just dismissed her remark and told her to live her life and not to be wasting it on stuff that was out of her control.

"A little knowledge could be a dangerous thing in the wrong hands," Lizzie had told her daughter, while she'd understood her concerns, she just couldn't go on living like that, her life would be a misery. Watching her husband, a sturdy six-foot man, progressively declining before her eyes was enough to be dealing with for now. She couldn't think any further than the day ahead. Elizabeth was now in a better place, things seemed to be going well with Tim, and Joe was keeping her busy. She seemed more accepting towards her dad's condition, less afraid of being in his company as Lizzie always thought she was. She'd seem distant at times but Lizzie always thought it was more she was nervous and afraid to be left alone with him. Even more so since he'd had the bad turn with his chest infection a while back.

Francis had earned a good pension from his army days so money was never an issue these days, every week like clockwork, it would go into their account. They'd always had a joint account not that Lizzie contributed much these days, in her nursing days she would have lodged as much if not more than Francis if she'd done nights.

Now, he still carried her although literally hardly able to carry himself.

He'd hidden her glasses under the sink, a place she wouldn't have looked for them in a million years had she not watched him do it, he was like the cat that got the cream. Picking them up from the table where she had been reading a letter she'd got in the post, as she went to the cooker, she spotted him going to the table and very discreetly putting them under his jumper and taking them to the sink, she'd let him off.

Chapter 7

Seemed content to sit and watch the TV after, she hadn't mentioned the incident nor would he remember it. Little peculiar happenings, all a part of his daily existence now. She'd begun to find different things in funny places, like a piece of pork wrapped in a handkerchief found on changing his bed under his pillow, a toy train belonging to Elizabeth's little Joe that he'd cried for, for days, thought to have dropped out of his buggy, was found in an old soup pot that only came out on the rare occasion that Lizzie took it into her head to make chicken soup. She'd found the remote control in the fridge after searching the house for it one day when the twins came round, thought the world had come to an end when they couldn't put the TV on. Maybe, she'd thought, these things happen to keep one's mind off what was really happening, coping mechanisms perhaps!

Jeffrey, next door had come in for a visit, Mark was just getting up to leave, "Having a bit of bother with the old lavatory these days, Mark…if you get a minute you might have a look…" Jeffrey pulled a chair up beside Francis who was beginning to nod off after his dinner.

"…and how are you my old friend…" Francis put his hand to his face and looked blankly at his friend, dribble on his chin from sleeping with his mouth open. Lizzie discreetly wiped his face with a handkerchief while distracting Jeffrey with handing him milk and sugar for his tea.

"Sure he's grand…aren't ya…" Lizzie took his hand down from his face and held it for a moment in hers, it was cold. No matter what the weather, Francis always insisted on having a fire lighting in the kitchen, however small. He would say it was welcoming and kept you company when you were alone.

He'd chatted with his friend for a while sometimes struggling to get the words out, and laughing at the fact that he'd forgotten what he'd had to say. Jeffrey would laugh along and put it down to their age.

They'd got along well, Francis had found a good friend in Jeffrey.

Mark shouted goodbye from the hall, "Will sort that out for you in the next day or two," he'd said to Jeffrey. "…have to take the boys swimming…it's all go…"

"Aw, sure there's no rush at all lad…no rush at all…"

"I was thinking of getting a dog…what do ya think Lizzie? Always had a dog in our house when we were growing up…no thoroughbreds mind…couple of mongrels…you know?" "Sure you'd get awful fond of them…might get me out walking a bit…the old hips are beginning to seize up on me…need to get them moving…be an awful thing if I couldn't do the garden…I'd be lost…"

"That would be lovely…" Lizzie remembered years ago when she was a child herself, and a neighbour's dog had pups. They used to go across, herself and Margaret, to see them every day, they were the most beautiful little things she had ever seen in her life. She'd begged and begged their mother to let them have one. Their neighbour, Mr Cahill had said he had homes for four of them so they could have the fifth one if they wanted it. She remembered it was brown and black with a white blob on his head. She wasn't quite sure if it had been a male or a female, that didn't matter back then, all she knew was it was all she wanted. When her mother had finally given in to them and said they could have the pup as long as it didn't get under her feet and they would clean up after it, there had been great excitement.

They'd gone to the corner shop to get a big box and made a comfortable bed for him (or her). Sure no one in the house got any sleep that night only listening to the puppy crying, her father had got up early the next day and got rid of the dog, they cried for days.

No one ever found out what became of it but often when he'd be in a bad mood after drinking the night before he would tease them and say he'd put a rock around his neck and drowned him. Lizzie often thought, not even he could have been that cruel, surely!

"What type of dog are you thinking of getting…" Jeffrey had polished off the whole packet of ginger nuts, Lizzie knew they were his favourites, she had to laugh.

"Aw sure I'm only thinking yet…we'll see…might even end up getting a bicycle…"

"Jeffrey you're a scream…" Lizzie always liked his company, always thought it was a gift that some people had, to make other people laugh, to lighten a situation, Jeffrey could do that.

As he got up to go, so did Francis, Lizzie walked with them down the hall to the front door and explained to Francis that Jeffrey had to go home and that he was already home. He laughed and Jeffrey shook hands with him and was off. "Let's go and watch a bit of TV…" she took him into the sitting room and went to turn on the TV, when she turned back to him, he had gone. She'd watched from the kitchen door to see him struggle to open the front door, they'd had locks fitted on the top of both front and back doors for safety. Something Francis didn't seem to remember so he couldn't get out. She'd wondered where he'd wanted to go. Did he just want to get out of the house or was he running from something? Her…perhaps or maybe himself, his mind must be a torment to him, she'd thought, lost, alone, goodness knows what he was feeling. At this stage, you could almost physically see his head was beginning to shrink, lose its shape, like everything inside was being crushed within. Probably her imagination, probably his weight loss, just looked like it to her.

His movement too, began to become very slow and almost painful looking, though if asked, if he was in any pain, he would just smile and say no, in a quiet gentle voice. Always gentle in his ways, wouldn't hear of anyone raising their voice for any reason. Many a time, Elizabeth would have been told to hush in the nicest possible way when she would take off on one of her rants.

Lizzie, having had such a different upbringing often envied her daughter having such a wonderful dad, but then, that was how it should have been, she'd thought, she'd just wondered at it.

Maisie was ecstatic at the other end of the phone, it had been eight years now since she'd left Harry. "Do you think it's too soon…will people talk…" She'd met Vincent at her bridge club, got chatting and became good friends, now Vincent wanted to be more than good friends.

“Look Maisie…people will always talk…wouldn’t you be worse to pay heed to them…sure they’ll tire of talking about you and they’ll crucify someone other poor creature…don’t be daft…if you can find a bit of happiness…I say grab it with both hands my friend…life is short.”

Lizzie had been friends with Maisie now for what must have been over forty years, she’d put up a lot with Harry, the best in the world but a martyr for the drink. There wasn’t a bit of harm in him but she’d been let down so many times. She might be all dressed up to go somewhere with him, having put in a lot of effort to look her best, and when they’d get there he would disappear to the bar. Maisie would end up going home on her own in a taxi. It took a lot of courage on her behalf to call it a day, leaving Harry all but bewildered as to why.

“He didn’t have a drinking problem…what would the neighbours think…”

She was well due a bit of happiness and Lizzie wished her all the luck in the world in trying to find it.

She would want a full report when Maisie came round for tea on Sunday.

Lizzie would get up early while Francis was sleeping and bake a cake for afternoon tea. Maisie would come with a bag of goodies as usual but a bit of homemade cake would go down very well. It could be baking away there while she looked after Francis.

Still wanting his own independence although now hardly able, Francis would toilet himself and shave with his new electric shaver. He thought it was the best thing since the sliced pan. She’d help him with dressing and tying his shoes but the bathroom was as yet of his own doing (except for the odd accidents in the night).

There was a lovely smell of baking coming from the kitchen, Lizzie was very pleased with herself having made the effort, and everything had to be planned now. Couldn't just decide to do a bit of baking out of the blue like she used to, though she did enjoy it. Nowadays, Francis and his needs had to come first, and of course his safety, if the oven was on, she would have to watch in case he would open the oven door and burn himself (again). She remembered he'd been looking for his glasses and opened the oven door that day, thinking they might be in there, he'd said. Had taken weeks to heal his poor hand, didn't seem to feel the pain of it but Lizzie thought it must be sore? It had blistered and wept for weeks; she'd been vigilant in keeping infection away.

Walking a step ahead of him, going down the stairs, Lizzie waited as Francis stopped half way, with sleep still in his eyes, he tried to get the words out, "A…a…nice…" She could tell by his smile that he was talking about the nice smell coming from the kitchen.

Maisie was prompt as usual, if she said four o clock, she would be standing on the doorstep at four o clock.

"Lizzie…I don't know if I'm doing right or wrong…sure I am a bit long in the tooth for romance…and all that…"

Seems Vincent had given her a lift home from her bridge club the weekend before and tried to kiss her, taken by shock she'd swiftly got out of the car looking back to say, "I'll be saying goodnight then…" And disappeared behind the bushes to find her keys and catch her breath.

He'd rung and apologised the next day and hoped he hadn't made things awkward for them, finishing the conversation with his wish that he would like them to be more than friends.

After three cups of tea and enough chat to have one's ears ringing for a week, Maisie got up to go, Francis had retired to the sitting room, (hadn't quite lost all of his senses yet!)

Lizzie felt refreshed, it had been too long since she'd spent that much time with her lifelong friend, far too long. They'd laughed, cried, joked. *Just like old times,* she'd thought, she'd needed that, she felt good.

Elizabeth was going to take a day trip and wondered if, Lizzie, would like to go along. "Be a break for you…" she'd said. "Tim will sit with Dad…"

Franie wanted to sit at the front of the train, Lizzie tried to explain to her that those seats were reserved for people who struggled to walk and that, she'd pointed to the sign, "Reserved for Disabled."

"Like Poppy…" She'd stuck Lizzie to the ground, she'd never really thought of Francis as being disabled, but she'd been right, he actually was. She wondered if he would be okay without her for the day. Tim was good with him, patient and kind, two of his biggest needs, someone to be patient and kind to him. She'd shed a silent tear and did her best to enjoy the day. It seemed to mean a lot to Elizabeth, made a fuss of her, treated her to a lovely lunch. Although Franie ended up wearing most of it as she insisted on sitting on her lap and proceeded to spill the coffee down on top of them both. Luckily gone cold as she hadn't had a chance to drink it. Everything seemed well when they got back, Tim had sat to watch TV with Francis and fallen off to sleep himself only to wake with a start realising he was to watch Francis, who was still snoozing, to his great relief. He'd had the table set for a cup of tea when they'd arrived. Lizzie sat without taking her coat off to rest her feet, having walked for miles around the shops, enjoyable as it was; it didn't do much for her poor bunions.

Chapter 8

Francis got up and started to help her to take her coat off. Was it his way of saying he'd missed her and didn't want her to go again and leave him? she'd wondered.

"I will never leave you my love…never." A day had obviously been too long. She hugged his frail body, almost able to feel his bones as she did, there was a time when she could barely breathe after they'd hug, he would hold her so tight. She'd not ever leave him again, not even for a moment, she was beginning to panic. He was failing a little bit every day. She was losing him.

Francis's sister Dee had rung while Lizzie was out, Tim had almost forgotten to say, had turned at the gate as he remembered.

"Didn't say what she wanted…said she'd ring you later."

"Wonder what that could be." Lizzie walked slowly down the hall from the front door, Francis walking ahead, he'd followed her to the door to see Elizabeth and Tim and the children off. Lizzie wasn't getting away this time, she thought to herself. He was watching her every move since she'd come in.

Dee was calling for a visit, she would be in town on Saturday to buy material to make new curtains, always handy with the sewing machine, and she would love to spend a little time with Francis if that wasn't an awkward time for them.

"Of course, Dee...sure you're welcome anytime...no need to call in advance..."

"Sure, I wouldn't walk in on anyone unannounced my dear. Let alone you and you up to your ears." Lizzie had smiled as she put the phone down, a real old fusspot Dee, but a heart of gold.

"My goodness...that town would put years on ya..." She'd huffed and puffed the whole way down the hall and sat with a sigh of relief.

"It's so nice to see you Dee. How's Bartley keeping..." Lizzie put the kettle on.

"Sure, what would be on any man..." Wiping the sweat from her brow, she went on to root in her bag left on the floor between her legs. "Don't know if I'm coming or going half the time these days...sweating...flustered...dropping things...sweating...I don't know...it's a man's world...no two ways about it, Lizzie...have you reached that strange time of life yet...you're a bit younger than me I suppose...be lucky to get out of it alive not to mind sane..." She wiped her brow with her handkerchief.

Francis had been sleeping in the sitting room, as he shuffled into the kitchen, Lizzie went over to assist him in sitting in his chair.

"Look who's come to visit..." He'd smiled at Dee as if he'd recognised her but Lizzie wasn't sure.

"Cup of tea..." She took his favourite mug from the cupboard and watched as Dee pulled her chair up right alongside him. Francis always did say you could never get a word in edgeways when Dee would be around and it was no different this time, he listened intently, occasionally looking over to Lizzie. A bit restless, by the time Dee had gotten up to leave. Lizzie had so enjoyed her visit though, showed her the lovely tweed material she had bought and the pattern she was going to cut out of it. She'd only gone in to buy material for curtains but had spotted some lovely tweed and would make a new skirt for herself.

"You're so gifted with sewing…aren't you?"

Lizzie had often struggled to thread a needle.

"Aw sure, it isn't rocket science…was bred into us in school…don't know if they do needlework in school at all these days. The old sewing machine is now beginning to creak like myself…couldn't be doing with those fancy ones…there's more gadgets on them…would confuse a saint…"

Mark had commented that Lizzie was looking tired and that maybe he would stay the odd night and let her sleep in the spare room to get a good night's sleep. Though he'd meant well, Lizzie wouldn't hear of it, she would be fine.

Minding Francis wasn't the strain that was causing her to lose sleep, the thought of losing him was what was wearing her out.

She'd wanted to watch him every moment of every day and night, losing sight only when the exhaustion made her give into the sleep, every moment precious. Every day, a day closer. She would waste no time on self-pity, she was no hero to the cause. She was just plain heartbroken, holding on for dear life, hoping someday…someday the fog might lift.

"Mam…I'm worried about you…" Mark was leaning on the kitchen worktop as Lizzie peeled the potatoes. *Nice mashed potatoes and a lamb chop,* she had thought to herself, Francis loved a bit of lamb.

He looked concerned. Lizzie knew she was looking a bit watery lately but she would be okay, a bit of fresh air, now that the evenings were getting a bit brighter, that would sort her out. Francis walked so slow, it would have to be a bit warmer before she would attempt to go walking with him.

"I'm right as rain son…right as rain…" She handed Mark the peelings of the potatoes and he took them outside to the bin.

He watched as his mother lifted the pot of potatoes onto the cooker, not knowing he was watching, she sighed and stood staring into the other room where his dad was sleeping in front of the TV. He wondered what she might be thinking, she was miles away. For a moment he had thought to himself that he had never really noticed the quiet before, the TV had been turned down and there was a sort of stillness, a loneliness.

Maybe it was because his house was always so full of life with the two boys constantly pulling toys from each other and Eilish shouting at the top of her voice. Such a pair of lungs on a toddler he'd never seen, to take the attention from the boys and over to herself.

No, he had never really noticed before, he would always call round as often as he could, *but was he giving them enough of his time?*

Lizzie would always ask if he wanted to stay for a bit of dinner, didn't matter if there were two or ten, if you called by and she was cooking there was always the invitation to stay. With their busy lives, she would understand when they seldom accepted the invitation, but always hoped they would. The house could be lonely at times.

Francis though present, was most of the time absent now, she remembered a time when there weren't enough hours in the day, days when she'd long to put her feet up.

Her eyes lit up when Mark said he would stay for dinner, she would set the table, something she didn't often do these days in the evening when there was just herself and Francis. Was easier to have a plate on their laps, it would be lovely to have the company.

They would have ice cream for dessert.

"Any word from Freddie...how's he getting on in the priesthood?"

Mark smirked. "Ya know, Mam...I still can't see Freddie as a priest...it seems unreal..." Lizzie took his plate over to the sink.

"See Mark...you don't always know someone like you think you do...do you?"

"That was delicious..." He looked at his watch and apologised to have to leave but it was near bedtime for the boys and they were a handful, Kitty would be wondering where he was. It was so nice to have him round, Lizzie knew he had places to be and she was grateful he had taken the time. *Just like Mark to be thoughtful,* she thought.

Elizabeth had worked herself into a tizzy, Tim came in from work to find her in tears. Franie's birthday was days away and when she had asked her what she wanted to do for her birthday, she had replied that she wanted to have her birthday cake in Poppy's house.

Elizabeth had thought that a bit strange and asked her why, to which she had replied, "Well poppy is a bit sick so…maybe we could cheer him up…you know how a birthday cake always makes everybody happy mummy…Poppy doesn't smile anymore…can we…please?"

"Whatever you want…" Elizabeth had held back the tears until she had gone happily on her way, but only just. She cried her fill and then some more, got herself into a state. Tim had just held her until she could tell him what had upset her, baby Joe had slept through it and Franie played away in the garden, oblivious to the upset her words had brought.

"I don't know if I can deal with this…I go round there…cheerful and light hearted…but inside…inside I just want to scream…Dad…Dad…but he doesn't know me Tim…he doesn't even know me now…" Tim held her tight, she was finding this harder than she had been letting on, fragile, broken and helpless.

She'd had so many regrets, been so selfish for so long, full of her own importance, so much wasted time. Now she would never have the chance to say she was sorry, so very sorry. She knew her mother knew her down to a tee, she knew she had blocked her out of her life for a long time and treated her disgracefully. Looking for attention from her dad constantly, criticising her efforts in looking after him when she was doing her best. Yet all she had shown her in return was love and kindness. It was too little too late but she would try to make it up to her, that was all she could do now.

"Poppy…will you help me to blow out the candles?" Franie was bursting with excitement, she had gone into the sitting room and taken Francis by the hand to blow out her candles. All dressed up in her party dress, she pulled him to his feet and proceeded to drag him across the room to where the cake was alight with candles.

"Isn't it the most beautiful cake Poppy…are you happy?"

She looked into his face to see him smile, it would have made her day.

"Poppy is so happy that you brought your cake round…so happy…aren't you Poppy?" Lizzie took him by the hand and sat him down, the exertion had made him pant.

Franie was very quiet on the journey back home in the car, Tim thought she had gone to sleep, looking in the mirror, he could see she hadn't.

"You okay birthday girl…worn out blowing out the candles?"

"Do you think Poppy will ever smile again?" Franie was staring out of the window as she spoke.

By the time the car came to a halt she had fallen asleep, a tear still wet on her little face.

Lizzie had looked after Francis when Elizabeth and Tim and the children had left, the excitement too much for him he hadn't made it to the bathroom on time. She knew there were adult disposable pants available but it seemed so degrading. Francis, a proud and sensitive man, how could she introduce such a thing to him. She would put that off as long as she could. Though there had been quite a few accidents of late, and she knew she was only putting off the inevitable.

She watched as he slept, comfortable and warm, she stroked his forehead and wanted to hold him tight. Just hold him tight like she used to. In each other's arms, they could have taken on the world. They'd struggled through so many ups and downs but always came through with their love intact. She'd known for many years she'd had something special in Francis, she'd known love so true that nothing could separate them, he was her world and she was his.

Chapter 9

Freddie was coming to visit, wondered if he could perhaps meet up with Mark for old time's sake.

"Wonder will he be different…you know…being a man of the cloth now…"

Mark read the letter to Kitty who was busy multitasking, cleaning up a mess Alfie and Seanie had managed to create at the breakfast table, which was nothing out of the ordinary, and at the same time comforting Eilish who was going through a bad time with a back tooth coming through.

"Why would he be any different…" Kitty poured some fresh corn flakes into Alfie's bowl with Eilish tugging out of her apron wanting full attention. "Going into the priesthood is hardly going to change his personality is it?" She picked Eilish up into her arms and cuddled her. "My poor baby…those bold teeth have you half killed."

Seanie and Alfie were into it again, she had only turned her back for a minute and they were throwing cornflakes at each other.

"Okay guys, enough messing up, go upstairs and get ready for school."

Mark had been doing sandwiches for their lunches, never one to raise his voice at the children, he would negotiate a deal while they would brush their teeth. “First out the door to the car gets to choose a cd.”

Mark loved his music, never a radio station playing in the car, always one of his favourite cd’s. Had the boys as bad as himself now wanting to choose the music if going anywhere in the car. It had worked a treat, they were up and out in a matter of minutes. Kitty sat in the armchair with a sigh of relief, there was bound to be another hissy fit in deciding who got there first but Mark would deal with it as Mark always would, calmly and fairly.

Eilish needed a little TLC, and reassurance that teething didn’t go on forever, it only felt that way.

She would take her to see Poppy once she’d tidied up. The kitchen was like a bomb hit it, as usual. All would be tidied up only to be as bad as ever once the boys returned from school later on. Who was it that said, “To tidy the house while the children are growing was like sweeping the snow while it was still snowing.”

Kitty couldn’t remember where she had heard that saying but they were the truest words ever spoken.

But sure she loved it, she loved every moment of her children growing, watched every emotion as they got more curious every day. She particularly loved the different expressions on their little faces that changed by the minute.

She would relish every moment, they were growing fast, time would come when they would go their own way but for now, they were the centre of her and Mark’s world.

She could never understand how anyone could ill-treat a child, any child let alone their own. She remembered when she was working, seemed a lifetime ago now, she worked with a girl who’d come in every day in a state. Married very young because she'd gotten pregnant, her father wouldn't hear of bringing up a child on her own, that boy would stand by her and support her and the child.

The biggest mistake of her life she would often say, treated her like a doormat, had no respect for her whatsoever, and as for her baby, a beautiful little girl. The stories she would tell Kitty would make her cringe sometimes. Ended up, he'd gone off for himself, got another poor girl pregnant and she hadn't seen sight nor light of him. Her dad who'd regretted forcing her into marriage, now realised she would have been better off raising that child on her own.

He was a waste of space and if he had anything to do with it, he would have nothing to do with his daughter or indeed his granddaughter again. Sometimes Kitty thought people don't know when they are blessed. An innocent child, only an animal would treat them badly, an animal.

Lizzie was so glad to see Kitty and Eilish come up the path, she had been cleaning the kitchen window.

"Could hardly see out." She lifted Eilish as she ran to her, still sniffling with one red cheek.

"We're having a bad day Nanny." Kitty rubbed Eilish's back as she snuggled into her Nannies arms.

"Poor dear…wonder if you might manage some ice cream."

It was the first time Kitty saw her smile all morning, usually such a cheerful little thing, she felt for her.

Francis had come down the hall to the front door, Eilish wriggled her way out of Lizzie's arms and ran to him.

"Poppy, I have a so tute."

She took Poppy's hand and walked him back into the kitchen and over to the fridge to get some ice cream.

“Poppy would you like ice cream for your so tute too?”

Francis rubbed his lips with his hand and folded his arms as if he was thinking about it. For a moment he stood still. Lizzie watched from the doorway, aware that he was confused, to avoid him getting upset, she walked towards him and fixed his glasses that had moved slightly down his nose. Seemed to be getting a bit loose. “There my good man…we’ll have to get Mark to tighten those for you.”

Eilish had managed to open her ice cream and was perched in front of the TV. Kitty stuck a tissue in her cardigan for the dribbles, no doubt there would be plenty and told her to mind Nanny’s couch. “How are you, Lizzie? Francis seems in good form.” Kitty pulled the chair out from under the table and plonked down, “It’s lovely to sit.”

“Sure, I’m grand…you look tired.” Lizzie had the kettle on the boil and was making her way to the fridge to get the milk.

“Oh, that’s because I am tired…Eilish is awake half the night with that tooth…she’s earned this one…poor thing. Mark must be half stupid at work as well today, he didn’t get much sleep either…said he’d call by later. Has to look at something for Jeffrey…something wrong with his toilet I think…is it…I don’t know.”

Lizzie remembered Jeffrey had asked Mark about something all right a couple of weeks before. “Cup of tea?”

Lizzie left the cup in front of Francis and sat down beside him, he reached for her hand and said, “Thanks,” nodding his head.

Lizzie placed her hand on top of his and replied, “It’s no bother at all my dear…no bother at all…”

“You’re keeping well Francis…” Kitty handed him the plate of biscuits, he nodded with a smile and took one and as she took the plate away, he grabbed her wrist and reached for another biscuit.

Jeffrey was insisting Mark take payment for repairing the toilet.

“Not at all…will you stop? If one can’t do a favour for a friend…what has this world come to?”

“You’re a good lad…” Jeffrey appreciated his help.

“Hi, anybody home?” As he walked into the kitchen, Mark could get a lovely smell. “Been baking, Mam…something smells lovely.”

“Aw, just a few fairy cakes, promised I’d do some for Eilish and the boys and send them round, when I heard you were calling to Jeffrey…knew you would be in.”

“You’re as good…” Mark kissed his mother on the forehead.

“Where’s Dad?”

“Fr Watters called by, was going to visit an old friend…your dad would have known him as well from his army days…only found that out the night of the army do a while back. Norman came over to say hello to your dad and sure when he saw Fr Watters, there was great excitement…had grown up in the same village it seems…small world.”

“That reminds me, Mam…Freddie’s coming to visit…”

“Freddie…aw, poor Freddie, it’s been a while. Saw his mum at the supermarket the other day…looks good. I’m sure she’s very proud of him…hadn’t had an easy time growing up…poor lad. I always liked Freddie…something very nice about him.”

Mark took the milk out of the fridge and sat at the table, always guaranteed a nice cup of tea when he called. He reached for the fairy cakes left on the table to cool, Lizzie tapped him on the hand. "They won't miss one, Mam…yum they're nice."

"Go on, better have another one…a bird will never fly on one wing…"

Lizzie handed him the plate. "Was thinking of taking Kitty and the kids on holiday this year, Mam…what do you think? Hate leaving you with Dad the way he is."

"Will you stop? Go off and enjoy your young family. Your dad and I have lived our lives…he'll be fine, don't be worrying."

"We used to take you and Elizabeth to the seaside on the holidays…your dad would book two weeks off and he'd be more excited than you would…I used to say to him, it's like I have three children with me sometimes."

"He'd want to take ye on all the rides…buy ye ice cream…I remember ye buried him in the sand one time and he closed his eyes when ye had finished and pretended he was dead…well you'd hear Elizabeth screaming all over the beach…aw, lovely memories Mark. These are your years to be making memories with your children…don't waste a minute."

Mark reached for his mother's hand across the table.

"Better get those fairy cakes in a bag before you eat them all."

Lizzie got up to go to the drawer and smiled at Mark, he too, was struggling to keep things as normal as possible.

"Do you remember when Dad used to take me fishing, Mam?"

Mark could see the happiness in her face as she re-visited the past, he wanted to take her back there again, they talked and laughed and reminisced and cried.

Fr Waters had pulled up outside and was helping Francis out of the front seat of the car, Mark had just left and said he would ring later to see that his dad had got home okay. Lizzie had stood at the window waiting and watching for his return, the house was so quiet without him, so empty.

"Cup of tea Father?"

Lizzie walked Francis down the hall and into the kitchen.

"Good day?" she opened Francis's shoes and put on his slippers.

"That's better…" Francis spoke in such a low gentle voice that it was almost faint.

He looked tired. Lizzie watched him as she left the priest to the door, he would have to rush off because he had a residents meeting and with a giggle he'd said, "Be jeepers, they'll have my guts for garters if I'm late."

He was so good-humoured, Lizzie thought and so thoughtful to remember Francis when he went to visit their mutual friend.

They'd had a lovely afternoon, Francis had begun to snooze in his chair by the time Lizzie had seen Fr Waters off, it didn't take much to exhaust him these days. She would let him sleep, have tea when he woke up.

"Freddie, my old friend. Come in come in." Mark was alone in the house when Freddie called. Kitty had taken the boys swimming and Eilish had insisted on going along. He'd promised her he'd put her favourite TV programme on, would give her a treat but no, nothing would please her only to go along with the boys. For peace sake, Kitty had decided to bring her along, she could watch as they had their lesson.

Chapter 10

Although it would be impossible to watch her, she knew while trying to get the boys dressed, but she would have to manage, anything for a quiet life. Mark would have gone along, only he'd made arrangements with Freddie, he would call to the house and have a catch up and maybe if it suited, they might go along and visit Mark's mam and dad. He'd said he would love to see them.

"So how are things…should I call you father or what…" They both laughed, "No, I'm still Freddie around here…it's great to be back. You don't realize how much you miss a place until you return sometimes."

"So, tell me all about it…what made you decide to…you know…take this route." Mark was hoping he wasn't being rude in asking.

"I don't know Mark…it just happened…I never really felt I fitted in anywhere you know, always felt out of place…went on retreat with a group from college then…and here I am…changed my life."

"Certainly, seems to be suiting you anyway." Mark pointed to his stomach, Freddie was always skinny growing up. Mark remembered his dad asking him what he'd had for lunch on a school day.

He'd only be home and he'd be round at Mark's again to walk back to school. "What did you have for lunch young fella…a run around the table?"

He could still see his dad sitting with them at the table, joking with Freddie. *Lots of water under the bridge since then,* Mark thought to himself, *and lots of tears shed.*

They talked for the best part of the afternoon, talked about old times, the funny things they'd gotten up to, the bullying that went on. Freddie seemed to remember the teasing and bullying. Funny how certain things stick in your memory. They even talked and laughed about old girlfriends. "Pity you missed Kitty and the children…they were only gone out the door when you came."

"Sure I'll see them again…be around for a while yet."

"Want to run over to visit the folks…or do you have time to? Can do it again if you're in a rush?"

"Love to…it's been a while…how's your dad doing? It's an awful debilitating condition…have a lady in the parish I'm in, with something similar…go to visit her on a regular basis. She used to do the flowers on the altar in the church. Sometimes, you do have to question God's ways…a lovely woman…so charitable…good living…I don't know, it's very testing at times…"

Mark had told his mother that he was expecting Freddie to call that afternoon, but he hadn't said they might drop by, so he thought he would ring her and let her know they were going to call.

"Sure, there's no need to be ringing…you're welcome to call anytime…be lovely to see Freddie. I'll put the kettle on."

Mark had to laugh at his mother, a cup of tea was the answer to everything and that it was. From the happiest of moments to the breaking of one's heart, there was always a great comfort in the cup of tea. Mark could see the expression on Freddie's face when he saw his dad, it was very hard to conceal it, and he'd obviously seen a big change in him. It was after all, a good few years since he'd called and sure Mark himself could see his dad failing by the day not to mind the years.

"Sit down there and tell us what you've been up to."

Lizzie could see the change in Freddie's expression as well, looking at a person day in day out you didn't really take much notice, she'd thought to herself, but it was different for Freddie, she understood.

Francis did his best to bless himself recognising, not the boy he'd known growing up but the fact that there was a priest present.

"Would you pray with him?" Lizzie knew Francis missed his prayers so much, she'd pray with him every morning and every night before going to bed but it wasn't the same for him, he'd forgotten the words of most of his prayers.

Seemed to have accepted it now but in the beginning, it would upset him when he couldn't remember. Lizzie used to say to him that words weren't necessary. "God knows. God knows everything my love." She'd comfort him and he'd trust in every word she'd say.

"It would be my honour to pray with you Francis…let's sit down."

Freddie took Francis by the arm and led him shuffling to the table to sit down. Mark went into the sitting room after his mother to find her standing in front of a photograph of his dad in uniform.

"Wasn't he a handsome man in his day…I remember that day well. Your grandmother…your dad's mother Emily had come to stay after your granddad…dad's father had died…he was after marching in the St Patrick's Day parade." She was smiling proudly. Mark felt a bit choked up looking out into the kitchen to where an old frail man was sitting with a priest, a shadow of his former self, hardly recognisable from the photo.

He wasn't going to upset his mother now.

"Sure, isn't he handsome still…" They laughed and hugged, both hurting as much as the other, both hearts bleeding inside.

Elizabeth came through the door like a gust of wind

"Freddie…"

She gave Freddie a hug and pulled out the chair beside him at the table, getting up again to give her dad a kiss on the forehead.

"How are you today, Dad? Telling Freddie all your sins…"

Francis smiled.

"Sure, what sin is on you my good man…and you carrying the biggest burden of all…" Freddie excused himself and asked if he could use the bathroom.

"Never changed…always asked if he could use the bathroom as often as she told him he didn't have to be asking, he would still ask…" Lizzie went to put a light on in the hall.

"It's dark enough in this hall…you might trip over something."

Freddie thanked her and she could see he was upset.

Elizabeth took a paper bag out of her handbag, she winked at her mother and gave it to her dad. Francis opened it awkwardly and held the framed photograph of Franie and baby Joe upside down. "This way, Dad…" Elizabeth turned the photograph the right way up.

"Who's this, Dad? Who's the little girl?" She pointed to Franie in the photograph but there was no response.

"Look at the baby, Dad…can you remember his name?"

Francis took the photograph and got up from the table. Lizzie was always nearby just in case he needed assistance. He shuffled his way into the sitting room and Elizabeth got up to follow him.

"No…leave him, Elizabeth…leave him for a minute."

Lizzie wanted to watch and see what he would do with the photograph, sure and certain he would hide it, she wanted to know where to find it later on. Mark got up from the table and Freddie had now returned from the bathroom with two red eyes, his glasses only highlighting the fact that he'd been crying.

Francis had sat in his chair in the sitting room and looked at the photograph for at least two minutes before he took out his handkerchief from his cardigan pocket and began to shine the glass. Elizabeth took her mother's hand and gasped, not one to hide her feelings Lizzie told her to hush.

She wiped her eyes only to have them fill with tears again. Francis had shined the glass of the photograph and kissed both children separately.

"I'm so sorry, Mam…I didn't mean for it to upset anyone…I just thought…"

"It's okay…shush now…don't want him to see you like this…go and talk to him…go on…" Lizzie herself was fighting to hold back the tears.

Freddie said his goodbyes and promised to call again before his departure, and he would be keeping them all in his prayers.

Mark went to say goodbye to his dad and told his mother he would be round later once he'd gotten the children to bed. He would give Kitty a break and look after them while she had a nice relaxing bath.

Both necessary and deserved, after the day she'd probably had at swimming.

Lizzie sat with Francis who was still holding the photograph.

"That's Franie and baby Joe…aren't they adorable?" She felt his hand as she reached to get the photograph, it was cold. Francis struggled to get them out but his words were very clear.

"Franie and Joe…I know, I know…" Lizzie pulled him into her and kissed him on the lips.

She wondered if maybe he'd like to stand it beside the TV where he could see it every day, but he wasn't parting with it, not yet anyway.

There was no rush, she would wait.

Maisie was calling for a visit, Vincent would be dropping her off and she wondered if it would be okay to maybe bring him in to introduce him, she'd hoped it wouldn't be cheeky of her.

Lizzie was delighted to hear, she was coming for a visit and would be even more delighted to meet Vincent, and it wasn't at all cheeky to ask. She would in fact look forward to it.

"Well…what do you think?"

Maisie sat patiently while Lizzie walked Fr Waters to the door, he'd been doing his weekly visits to the sick in the community and had called to see Francis. Was just walking up the path when Maisie and Vincent had pulled up outside. Assuring Fr Waters that it was perfectly okay to go on in and see Francis, Lizzie turned round to greet her friend.

"It's so lovely to meet you at last Vincent…won't you come in and have a cup of tea?"

Vincent had apologised for having to rush off but assured Lizzie they would call again and have that cup of tea.

His visit over, Lizzie walked the priest to the door and bid him goodbye.

"I'm sorry Maisie…you know you wouldn't see one all week and then everybody comes together…what harm…"

"He sure does go on a bit…that Fr Waters…doesn't he? Thought he was here for the day…" Maisie laughed.

"Maisie, you're a devil…poor Fr Waters, sure he's only doing his job…"

"Well…what did you think of Vincent…"

"He seems a really nice fella…has nice manners too…and not too hard on the eye either…for an old fella…"

Lizzie loved to tease Maisie, always took it lightly, herself and Lizzie went back a bit, she knew there was no offence intended and certainly none taken.

Francis slept contently on his chair in the sitting room after his visit from Fr Waters. He loved to chat with him, say a few prayers and maybe have confession, seemed to bring him ease and a sort of peace.

"Lizzie…I was just thinking…do you remember the fun we used to have years ago…looking at fella's and wondering if they were going to ask us to dance at the dances…God, I used to love the dances…the bands…”

“Yes, those were the days alright Maisie…but sure I’d nearly have to push you out on the dance floor if a fella asked you to dance…talk about shy…you were desperate…I don’t know how you ever got to get married at all…poor Harry…he was a nice man too…before…well…before he got too fond of the bottle…you know…sorry maybe I shouldn’t have brought that up…wasn’t very sensitive of me…”

“Sure, you’re okay…everybody knows he was a waster…mind you…there was a time…aw, sure, water under the bridge now…water under the bridge…I have good memories too…but mostly bad.”

Chapter 11

Maisie moved nearer to the table and leaned forward towards Lizzie.

"You know, Lizzie, God forgive me but I used to pretend I was asleep half the times when he'd come in from the pub at all hours…had to, otherwise he'd be wanting…you know what…told me one night it was his marital right…"

"He didn't force himself on you Maisie…surely not?"

"Aw…more often than I care to remember…wouldn't remember a bit of it then the next day…was the blessings of God himself we never had children…bringing children into a life of drink and arguing…"

Lizzie was in shock, Maisie had moved a bit away after she'd got married and though they never lost touch they weren't as in touch as they used to be. She remembered a time when one wouldn't sneeze without the other getting a cold, they were as close as sisters, closer even. After Maisie had left, sorry that Francis had slept through her visit and she didn't get a chance to chat to him, Lizzie sat for a while and let her memories take over.

Francis was very fond of Maisie, he'd have to have been or Lizzie would have been in a bit of a fix as they used to take Maisie out dancing with them many time. Lizzie always felt she was letting her friend down otherwise. After all, before Francis came along, they'd gone everywhere together, the cinema, the dances, shopping. She even had to go and sit in a courthouse once with Maisie when she'd been called for jury service. Otherwise, she wasn't going and would have gotten a fine, she was so backward and shy. Lizzie could never really understand why she'd had no confidence in herself.

Looking back, Lizzie thought Francis was such a patient man, never complained that Maisie would tag along, and always made her feel welcome.

It had been at a New Year's Eve party that Maisie had met Harry, she'd wanted Lizzie to go off on her own with Francis and enjoy herself.

"I'll be fine here…sit down with a book and you go off…it's not fair on Francis…me always tagging along…go on, off with you…"

Lizzie had dragged her off the chair and picked out one of her best dresses out of the wardrobe.

"It's New Year's Eve…you have to go dancing…we always go dancing on New Year's Eve…"

Didn't take much persuasion, it wasn't long before Maisie had perked up and was looking like a film star, turned out, it was to be the night she would meet her future husband.

Lizzie and Francis had danced all night, walked home in the early hours and kissed at the gate, he was such a gentleman in every aspect of the word. It was their wedding night that they had first made love, even back then, that was unusual. Francis respected that she'd wanted to wait and there was never any question about it, although at times, she had to admit it was hard, she had longed to be with him and he with her but they would wait. Maybe that was what held them together all those years, maybe respect for each other is the tie that binds.

Whatever it was, she knew she loved him now as much, if not more that the day they had married, and she was sure that in his heart, he would be feeling the same. Nothing could destroy that feeling, not even the soul-destroying illness that was stealing him away little by little every day. *Not even that,* she'd thought, *not even that.* She wiped her eyes and got up to start the dinner, she would not give in to the loneliness today, Francis would be awake soon, all was well.

Freddie's visit was nearing its end and he wondered if it was okay to call to see Francis and Lizzie before he left.

Francis had had a bad night, wandering around the house, wanting to go outside at four o'clock in the morning. Lizzie was exhausted when morning came, she had persuaded him to go back to bed and promised sincerely she would go walking with him first thing in the morning.

She'd left him in bed to catch up on his sleep, there was no point in telling Mark now, he would only make a fuss, and Elizabeth would only worry.

"Of course it's okay…he's more than welcome." She hung up the phone and hoped Mark hadn't sensed anything was wrong, he was so tuned in, she had to be very careful with her tone of voice, she'd made it as cheerful as she could.

It was afternoon when Freddie called. "Off first thing in the morning…don't know where the few weeks have gone…it's been lovely seeing everybody…" They'd chatted for a while before Mark arrived, he'd been caught up in a job and couldn't get away as early as he'd hoped.

"Aw sure, what harm…these things happen…sure, Lizzie and Francis are keeping me in chat here…isn't that right Francis…"

Freddie took Francis's hand from across the table and Francis put his other hand on top of Freddie's, he nodded and said, "God bless you."

When he took his hand away again, he'd left some money on Freddie's hand, not in it, but on top of it.

"Francis…what's this?"

Lizzie looked on. "Take it Freddie…he wants you to have it…we'd often walk to the chapel and he'll always put money in the box to light candles…sometimes more than we can afford…but that only happened once now in fairness. I keep an eye on him since…it's just something he likes to do…something he's still able to, I suppose."

"I will light some candles for you and Lizzie, Francis…okay…thank you so much…it's very generous of you…"

Francis smiled, he had a lovely smile, he seemed pleased.

"Heading off tomorrow so…" Mark buttered a scone, freshly baked in the morning, Lizzie found baking sort of therapeutic these days, when Francis would have his nap she would often take down her old box of recipes, wasn't ever very ambitious but could do a nice fruit cake or a decent enough scone she thought, never got any complaints anyway.

"Ya, I was just saying, don't know where the time has gone…it just flies by…enjoyed it though…and sure I'll be back…"

"Was saying to Mam, I was thinking of taking Kitty and the children on holiday…go to the seaside maybe for a few days…are you sure you can manage without me for a few days, Mam?"

Mark was always so concerned and thoughtful.

"Will you go off and enjoy yourselves…they'll only be small for a while…isn't that right Freddie? Life is short…I'll be just fine with your father."

Lizzie was glad she hadn't made a big deal of Francis's wandering around the house the night before, she quietly hoped it would never happen again, his absent stare always scared her, especially at night. She never really understood why but everything always seemed worse in the night. Even as a child, the darkness always brought a scary eerie feeling. Mark would have no notion of going on holiday if he knew, not a hope. He deserved the break and it would be lovely for Kitty and the children as well, she would cope.

Elizabeth had left baby Joe at home with Tim while she'd taken Franie to get new shoes. "She's growing like a weed this one…and a right little madam she's turning out to be…wanted the most expensive shoes in the shop…nearly had a fit when I wouldn't get them for her…sure where would she be going and she only knee high to a grasshopper…" Elizabeth left her bags on the chair and headed to the bathroom

"Thought I'd never get back…couldn't be queuing for a toilet in town…"

Franie went into the sitting room where Francis was sitting, watching the TV, climbed up on his lap and took his arm and wrapped around her.

Lizzie thought it was so cute how fond of her grandfather she was, when Elizabeth went to check on her ten minutes later, they were both asleep, "She'll break my heart. I'm thinking…she's so determined for a little person…" she looked over at her mother and they both smiled.

"I know…I know…she's not taking it from the wind…little madam…"

Elizabeth sat quietly looking out of the window.

"A penny for them…" Lizzie passed her the plate of biscuits.

"Aw! I'm miles away…just thinking Mam…Dad never really abused himself did he…I mean he never drank too much and he never smoked did he? I don't remember him smoking anyway…you'd wonder what brought on this awful disease wouldn't ya? Doesn't make sense…"

Lizzie had often wondered herself, was it anything in the food they eat, was it this, was it that was it the other? But sure, there were never any answers. Just plain bad luck, she thought, her lovely Francis a victim of pure bad luck.

"I don't know Elizabeth…sure you could drive yourself loopy thinking and wondering…be all the same. It is what it is now…we have to make the best of it…we still have your dad and we still laugh…it's not all bad."

"Wish I could think like that, Mam…I can't sleep at night…my mind is a torment to me sometimes…" Elizabeth started to cry.

"Shush now…you'll wake them…Elizabeth, love…I know nowadays people…well not all people either…but some people don't accept that some things are just God's will…you know your dad and I have our faith to keep us strong…and to be honest love, I don't think I could cope without it…God will provide…just have to trust in Him."

"...that's our belief. He's looked after us all these years...we won't give up on Him now...when we need him the most..."

Lizzie watched as her daughter tried to take it all in, as children, they were brought to mass, said their prayers before bedtime with them, but as they grew up, they would have to decide for themselves Francis used to say, "Don't worry they'll find their own way back if they stray..."

He'd often say to Lizzie if she worried that Elizabeth didn't get up for mass on a Sunday or Mark would say he was too busy to take time off to go to mass. She could still see Francis looking over his reading glasses and quietly continuing to read his Sunday paper, muttering as he did.

"Someday...they too, will find their God...and realise that he was there all along..."

"Aw, there you are..." Elizabeth picked Franie up on her lap as she wobbled into the kitchen still half asleep, her little face bearing the imprint of a button on her Poppy's cardigan where she must have been leaning on it while sleeping.

Lizzie gave her a drink of juice and went to check on Francis, still sleeping she decided to leave him.

"Sleeping a lot these days...suppose he gets bored too...a big change when you think of it isn't it...he was always so active...couldn't sit for a minute. I used to say to him...will you give your food a chance to digest? He'd be up from the table like a shot after the dinner...of course he'd just smile and give me a hug in passing."

Lizzie seemed thoughtful for a moment as Elizabeth zipped up the front of Franie's jacket. "Better get you home missy...Dad will think we eloped...see ya Mam...ring you later." She went in to say goodbye to her dad while Franie followed behind sucking her thumb.

"Bye bye, Poppy…I love you…" Franie kissed Francis's hand and he woke up. He looked up at Elizabeth, a dribble going down the side of his mouth. She kissed the top of his head and lifted Franie to go.

Chapter 12

When Lizzie came in from the front door after waving Elizabeth and Franie off, Francis was standing up. He'd had an accident while sleeping and struggled to get the words out.

"It's okay my love…it's okay…we'll get you sorted…"

They walked down the hallway and slowly up the stairs. One-step and a rest then the next step and a rest. Francis would sometimes sit down at the top of the stairs and it was impossible to get him up. Lizzie hoped today that he wouldn't do that, it was getting so hard, as much as she hated to admit it, she was struggling these days especially with the stairs. Once she had gotten him into the shower and into some fresh clothes, she thought maybe they'd go for a walk down the road, it was a lovely day.

Jeffrey was mowing the lawn as they passed.

"Ah, is it yourself, Francis?"

He came to the gate and chatted for a while.

"Better let you get on with the work…" Lizzie walked on and Francis saluted Jeffrey as they went. They walked to the chapel and to the grotto and back home again. It was a lovely break from the house for him, Lizzie thought we'll do that again tomorrow.

Helping Francis into bed that night, she noticed his ankles were a bit swollen, he hadn't complained of them being sore or anything but she thought they must be painful. Maybe the walk was too much for him, perhaps she'd wait a couple of days and see before they go wandering again. There was always that moment before he went to sleep, it was as if he…as if he was her old Francis again, just for a moment, he'd hold her as she leaned down to kiss him goodnight.

Maybe she'd wanted it so badly that she'd imagined it. She watched as he slept, so peaceful. If only things could be the way they were…if only.

She picked up the washing off the floor and put it straight into the machine. *Tomorrow is another day we must struggle on,* she'd thought.

As they sat at the back of the chapel at Sunday mass, Lizzie noticed Francis was getting a bit fidgety, she took his hand to reassure him but he got up to go. Jeffrey had been standing at the back of the chapel and held the door open for them as they approached.

"Everything okay?" Jeffrey followed them outside and helped Francis down the steps.

"I'm not sure…think he's a bit hot maybe…we'll get a bit of air and maybe we'll go back in…thanks Jeffrey…go on in you we'll be grand."

"Sure, I was only waiting for a chance to sneak off…honest to goodness but Fr Waters does go on a bit…doesn't he?"

"…I'll walk back with ye…sure maybe have an old cuppa and a chat…what do you think Francis?"

Francis was walking faster than Lizzie had seen him in a while, seemed to be in a hurry, maybe he wanted the toilet she thought. Although that was the last thing they would tend to before they left the house, always. She had to smile at Jeffrey though it wasn't a very nice thing to say about Fr Waters, true as it may be.

"Come on in Jeffrey…I'll put the kettle on…" Lizzie led Francis to the kitchen to sit down, looking back at Jeffrey as he came up the hallway, she hadn't realised that Francis was about to sit on the chair as she began to pull it out a bit to make more space for him, he'd missed the seat and sat on the floor. Lizzie began to laugh and proceeded to pick him up while Jeffrey came running in from the hall. Francis wasn't amused; he pushed Lizzie out of the way and she stumbled and fell against the cupboard, scraping her elbow as she went down. Jeffrey had managed to lift Francis up off the floor and sit him on the chair.

"Are you okay, Lizzie…are you sure?"

Lizzie had never expected that reaction but maybe she shouldn't have laughed, she didn't mean anything by it, it was just an automatic thing. Seemed funny at the time, she'd never seen that look of anger before, not with Francis.

Of course in working with older people while nursing all that time ago, she'd seen plenty of agitation and aggression and all that goes with Alzheimer's, why did she think it would be any different with Francis?

So many different patients, old and not so old, same traits.

"I'm fine Jeffrey…are you okay my love? I'm so sorry…I wasn't looking." Lizzie held her arms around Francis and she could feel the tension leaving his body, why was he so tense today what was so different between today and yesterday. His disease was progressing and more than likely. He would be doing his best to hide it from her, he'd never wanted her to worry about anything. She remembered how hard he would work and all the long hours he'd put in when the children were small and she'd given up her job, just to make ends meet. Things were tight enough, bills coming through the door, she used to hate to see the postman come in the gate, it was seldom good news, always a bill to pay. Barely bringing in enough to cover the food and electricity, Francis would take her hand, she still remembered that look on his face.

"Don't worry…we'll get there…" he'd say sincerely and she wouldn't worry and they would get there, always got through…that was many years ago now…before the fog.

She knew Francis better than he knew himself, the pain in his face would be him trying to break free of this torment that encaged him, he would be trying to lose the shackles that now held him in this awful place that prevented him from reaching out to her.

From loving her like he used to, from reassuring her not to worry.

Lizzie asked Jeffrey not to mention her falling over to Mark, he would only worry.

"Sure why would I, Lizzie…why would I? You take care now…you know where I am if you or Francis should need anything…" As he turned back at the gate, he laughed.

"Fr Waters will be down on his collection today…" Lizzie had to laugh.

The twins were so excited they couldn't sit off on holiday for two weeks in the sun. *How lovely,* Lizzie thought, *and so well-deserved.*

Mark worked hard, he was a good father and a very good husband, Kitty only had to mention she'd like something for the house and he'd be planning it for her next birthday or their wedding anniversary.

Put Lizzie in mind of Francis when he was a young dad, he, so doted on his children, never leaving her out either. He would take them shopping when it was coming up to her birthday and swear them to secrecy so that it would be a surprise, but sure Elizabeth would be only in the door and she'd be asking Lizzie what she thought they'd bought her for her birthday. Bursting to tell her and Mark threatening her that he would tell Dad. Francis enjoyed their banter often finding it difficult to keep a serious face with Elizabeth, Lizzie always thought he'd seen a lot of Elizabeth in Franie. Same mischievous look on her face, the odd tantrum thrown in, sure the apple doesn't fall far from the tree they say. Now Francis barely acknowledged their presence.

Lizzie wondered if maybe Franie could see the change in her Poppy, no more feeding the ducks, no more teaching her to tie her shoes, not much of anything really. Yet she always insisted on being near him, talking to him, snuggling up to him while he slept on the chair.

Elizabeth had told her that Franie had prayed for her Poppy every night before she'd go to sleep. At times, she would stand at the bedroom door and listen. "I think my poppy is very sad. Holy God, will you see what is making him sad and fix it so that he can be smiley again…I promise I will be so good…"

Elizabeth would hold her tears until she'd got down the stairs, it was so tough at times, she'd said.

Lizzie walked Francis to the front door to say goodbye to Mark and Kitty and the children, they were bubbling over with excitement.

"You sure you will be okay Mam…" Mark hugged his mother affectionately, and then his dad.

She wasn't about to tell him she would miss him every moment, and she would, or that she feared the worst might happen while he was away, because it might, she would smile and wish them well.

Mark was the type you could always depend on, you didn't have to call him, at times, it was like he could read her mind. She'd be wishing he would call by and there he'd be standing at the door, it was weird sometimes but she was always glad to see him.

Elizabeth had promised Mark that she would call every day while they were away, and she did, if only to put her feet up and drink coffee. But at least she was there; she was company for Lizzie and Francis too.

Joe was beginning to crawl around the floor, he was such a beautiful baby, very different in looks to Franie. Lizzie often wondered if his father was from around these parts?

Elizabeth had never mentioned Joe's dad or the night she'd gotten so drunk that she didn't remember who'd she'd been with. *An awful state of affairs altogether,* Lizzie thought. Looking at Francis, holding Franie's doll while she brushed her hair and struggling to put a ponytail in it, Lizzie had to smile. Not long now before she'd lose her patience and throw the doll and the hairbrush and all that goes with it across the room, she had such a temper.

Francis as gentle as ever would look on.

"Might take Joe to feed the ducks…want to come Franie?"

Elizabeth went into the kitchen to get some bread.

“C’mon Poppy…” Franie was pulling Francis out of his chair.

“C’mon Poppy.” Elizabeth put Joe into his pram and took Franie’s coat into the sitting room to put it on her.

“Poppy might be too tired today…here, put your coat on…”

Franie started to cry. “I want Poppy to come and feed the ducks…”

Lizzie wasn’t sure that was such a good idea.

“He’ll be fine Mam…he can hold Franie’s hand…be back in a few minutes again…give you a break…”

Lizzie watched as they walked to the end of the road, there wasn’t far to go but she still worried. Elizabeth had her hands full with the pram and Franie as well, how could she manage to watch Francis, but she insisted it would be fine. Lizzie had bread in the oven and couldn’t leave it for another ten minutes, when it would be done, she would follow them down and walk back with them.

She sat and put her feet up while she was waiting for the bread to finish baking, the smell of burning woke her nearly an hour later.

She’d fallen asleep in that short time, she knew she was exhausted but that had never happened before. The bread was burnt to a crisp, she was furious with herself, and where were Elizabeth and Francis.

She put her coat on and took off down the road to where they were to feed the ducks, there was no sign of them, she was really worried now.

Maybe they’d gone to the shop for sweets, maybe something happened while she’d been sleeping, where would she look.

“Mam…I just turned my back for a minute to watch Franie…and when I looked around, he was gone…I’m so sorry…where could he be?” Elizabeth was pushing the pram frantically with Franie holding on for dear life. “I was just coming back to tell you…I’ve looked all over…”

Chapter 13

Lizzie told Elizabeth to calm down that everything would be okay, at least she'd hoped it would.

"What if something's happened to him…what if?"

Franie looked on, white with fear, Joe had fallen asleep in his pram.

"Take the children back…I'll get Jeffrey to bring me around in the car to look for him…we'll find him, don't be worrying now…"

Jeffrey was only too happy to be of help, they drove all around the area, went to the chapel, the grotto, even called in to a few of the neighbours.

Although Lizzie was sure if he'd turned up at anyone's door, they would have contacted her straight away, it wouldn't be like him to be out on his own, not now. There was no sign of him.

Soon, it would be getting dark, she'd thought, and it had gotten a bit cooler as well, he wasn't wearing a coat. Elizabeth had struggled to put his coat on earlier and decided in the end that he didn't want to wear a coat.

"Let's go back to where they were feeding the ducks…never know he might have gone back that way…" Jeffrey was so good.

There was a bit of a commotion as they approached, Lizzie's heart sank, she couldn't get near enough to see so she asked a lady that was coming away from the crowd.

"Aw, it's so sad…must have fallen in…say he's a goner…"

Lizzie couldn't bear it, she pushed her way through, there was a body covered with a blanket from the ambulance. They'd gone back to get the stretcher; Lizzie wasn't allowed to go any nearer.

"Was it her Francis, did he fall into the water, was he…"

"Lizzie…Lizzie…" Jeffrey had been shouting at her but she didn't hear him, she had been frozen to the ground.

"Lizzie…" Jeffrey came up behind her as she looked on to what she thought was the remains of her beloved Francis.

"It's okay, Lizzie…Francis is okay…I had to lock him in the car to come and find you…in case the Lord bless us and save he'd go again on us…what happened here?"

Jeffrey could see that Lizzie had had a shock.

"Francis…oh Francis…I thought…" Lizzie hugged Francis and cried with relief the whole way back.

"Wouldn't want too many of them frights…eh." Jeffrey walked him home with a very grateful Lizzie.

"Poppy…Poppy…" Franie hung out of his leg and cried and cried.

Francis had been sitting under the wall in the park across from where they were feeding the ducks, he hadn't gone far. Was disorientated and had sat on the grass, Jeffrey had noticed a few gathering as they drove by so went to check it out just in case, as Lizzie went the other way. None the worse for his adventure, all were so relieved to see him sitting in his chair as darkness fell and it was time to get the children home to bed.

"I'm so sorry, Mam..." Elizabeth gave her dad a kiss on the top of his head softly so as not to wake him and said goodnight to her mother at the door.

"It's okay...all's well that ends well..." Lizzie gave her a hug.

Sitting down beside Francis she thanked her lucky stars, his wasn't the body wrapped up in a blanket that evening. *Bad news for somebody,* she'd thought, she'd felt so blessed.

It had rained all day and Francis was very agitated, Lizzie put the TV on but there seemed to be no interest whatsoever today. Sitting beside him on the sofa she thought his neck looked very thin.

In fact he was looking thin all over, she thought. *Looking at him every day, you don't tend to notice,* she'd thought to herself, but he had failed so much, it was heart wrenching looking at him. She would make a pot of tea and sit with him. She recalled her grandmother would say

"If anything, wait...let the work wait."

Today, she would let the work wait.

Twiddling with his jumper, he'd sat patiently while she'd made the tea, maybe he would like to look at some photographs, she'd read somewhere it was good for the memory to look at photographs.

She climbed up on the chair to reach their photo album, now gathering dust on top of the china cabinet. She blew the dust off and sat down beside Francis on the sofa.

"Do you remember this?" She opened the first page of the album, there was a photograph of their wedding day, she remembered Francis's sister Sarah had given them the album after they'd come back from honeymoon and had the wedding photograph in it when they opened it. Back then not many could afford such a luxury but of course Sarah being posh in her ways had thought this was an ideal gift, and it was, it held so many memories now. They wouldn't have had a camera themselves but anytime they'd had an occasion, someone would have taken a photograph. Francis seemed to be taking an interest He smiled as she turned the pages, photographs of the children on their first day at school taken by a parent and given to them when they'd have met again at the school. Communion day, confirmation day the same. As Lizzie turned a page to a photograph of his mother and father, Francis began to cry, not really sure why, she'd thought maybe that was enough for one day, they would do it again. Not able to express his feelings, to cry was nowadays the only way she had of knowing something wasn't right, other than anger. He was beginning to show anger more frequently lately. She would leave him to rest a while.

As she prepared dinner, she glanced every now and then into the room to see if he was okay, he had fallen asleep. Lizzie sat at the kitchen table and continued to look at the album, the house was so quiet you could hear a pin drop. There was a photograph of Mark and Elizabeth playing in the sand, she remembered Francis's sister Sarah had taken them on a day trip for a treat to the seaside, they were so excited you'd think they were going to America, Francis had said.

Sarah had never had children of her own, Lizzie remembered when they'd got home, she had remarked on how mischievous Elizabeth had been she'd run into the sea without asking and Sarah couldn't catch up with her, got her clothes all wet, she was furious with her.

When Lizzie had turned the next page, it brought tears to her eyes.

It was from way back, she'd thought it must have been Maisie that had taken the photograph, Harry was in it too. It had been before they were even married, she remembered that dress, Francis always said the colour suited her. "But then…" he had said, "When you're beautiful, you would look good in a sack." She remembered she'd blushed.

Wonderful times, they'd gone on a boat trip, poor Maisie had been sea sick the whole way, they hadn't left the dock and she was green in the face. "I'll be fine once I get my sea legs…be fine." and she'd disappeared to the toilets, not to be seen again until they landed. She was so funny, up to all kinds. Francis was very fond of Maisie, Harry too, they'd had such fun together. Once, she remembered, when Maisie first started going out with Harry and he used to drink far too much back then as well, he'd fallen asleep after they'd been out and Maisie had tied his shoelaces together. Harry woke up full of the joys only to fall out on his face when he tried to get up. Maisie thought it was hilarious. His drinking problem didn't really seem too much of a problem back then, it was only when they'd gotten married and his drinking meant the bills were all left to Maisie to sort out, along with all that went with it.

Lizzie thought she'd better put the album away and get dinner served. Francis would be awake soon and he would need her.

As she watched while setting the table for dinner, Lizzie could see Francis was really struggling to get off the sofa, he'd got up and fallen back down again, he'd laughed to himself.

“Come on you…” Lizzie had made light of the situation and went along with it. “Dinner’s ready.”

She’d sat him at the table where he’d always sat but he got up and shuffled his way to the other side, not a thing he would usually do, she’d thought, but it was okay she would set the table over there for him.

“Your husband’s condition has deteriorated, Lizzie, since I saw him last…how are you managing?”

Francis’s doctor had called by to check him over to see if he needed anything. “We’re doing okay…aren’t we Francis…” Lizzie took his hand and he agreed smiling, there was a dribble coming down his chin. She wiped it as the doctor proceeded to write some sort of prescription.

“I’m going to give him something to relax him…help him sleep at night…”

Lizzie didn’t like the thought of having him medicated, he was restless at night sometimes but that was okay, she thought to herself, she would hold off and see how things would go. She was going to keep what was left of her husband for as long as she could. She wasn’t going to medicate him to make life easy for herself. She’d thanked the doctor and he was on his way. Francis oblivious to it all smiled as she came back into the kitchen. “You okay my love…can I get you anything?”

By now, she was beginning to recognise the signs. If he was in a giggly mood, you could expect a bout of anger at any minute, his eyes were dancing in his head and he laughed out loud, she would have a difficult day ahead.

Mark was due home from his holidays, he had phoned every single day since he’d left, some days Lizzie had lied she was ashamed to say when he’d asked about his dad. She would be so glad to have him home she'd missed him so much, she reckoned Francis had missed him too. Jeffrey had called in the day before and as he came into the kitchen, Francis seemed to be looking behind him as if he was expecting someone else, yes she thought he had missed him too.

"How's my favourite mother…" Mark looked very well with his lovely tan, looked much rested, he'd needed the break and it had done him good. The twins followed after, never able to walk in, always like a gust of wind the pair of them. Lizzie smiled, it was so nice to have a bit of life about the place again, it had been so quiet.

Elizabeth had had a tip in the car, was distracted by the children in the back and ran into the car in front at the traffic lights.

"Franie wouldn't put on her seatbelt…looked around for a split second…the lights must have changed…stop…got an awful fright…Joe was asleep luckily enough…woke him but he was okay…"

Lizzie took Joe from Elizabeth and told her to sit down, she looked pale with fright. Franie was still crying and wanted to sit on her mother's knee, Elizabeth started to cry.

"It'll be okay love…don't worry…long as you're all okay…be worse if there was someone hurt…come on now, don't upset the children…"

"I'm pregnant, Mam…what if?" Elizabeth wiped her eyes and told Franie that mummy had to go to the bathroom. Franie sucked her thumb and with eyes glued to the bathroom door continued to sniffle. *Poor thing,* Lizzie thought. She must have got an awful fright. She'd had no idea Elizabeth was pregnant, she couldn't be very far-gone she'd thought, making the situation even more worrying.

Chapter 14

"I'm bleeding, Mam…I haven't even told Tim yet and I'm going to lose it." Elizabeth was shaking with fright.

"Sit down…it will be okay…babies are well protected…you may not have lost it…let's not put the cart before the horse now…"

"God is punishing me…I know he is…" Elizabeth caught her breath and continued, "For all the bad things I've done Mam…I was a horrible person…it's my own fault…I deserve it…"

Lizzie put baby Joe into the high chair and put her arms around her daughter. "Stop now…we don't know if anything is wrong…I'll ring Tim."

Within ten minutes, Elizabeth was on her way to the hospital. Tim was devastated by the news, he'd had no idea Elizabeth had been pregnant.

"Why didn't you say something…you're lifting Joe and Franie…" Taking her hand in his, he reassured her everything would be okay.

Elizabeth's condition was monitored and she was sent home to take it easy. She'd been very lucky and she would have to take things very easy for a while, all was well with the baby.

Mark was at Lizzie's when they returned. Lizzie had rung him after they'd left and asked if he wouldn't mind keeping an eye on his dad while she tended to the children. Franie was still sobbing when they got back.

"Well, I believe congratulations are in order…" Mark hugged Elizabeth as she came up the hallway. "You did half give us a fright though."

Elizabeth looked exhausted, worn out between the shock and the worry. After a nice cup of tea and a chat, all seemed well again.

"Dr Canavan was asking for Dad…said he'd called by the other day…you never said…" Elizabeth was being monitored by her GP after the tip, having the same GP since she was a child. Dr Canavan was the family doctor.

"Yes, he called by there one evening, said he was passing…wanted to check your dad out…" Lizzie had no intention of telling them in case they would worry she told her.

"He'd spoken about Alzheimer's though not directly about Dad ...with patient confidentiality and that but…it scares me, Mam…it's like he's just…I don't know…fading away…"

Elizabeth looked so concerned and heartbroken.

"…if only there was something we could do…anything to stop this thing…there's no coming back from this, Mam…is there? How do you cope? Sometimes I think I'm going crazy…"

Lizzie reassured her that everything that could be done was being done and that sometimes she too got scared, wanted to shout out, cried, all of the above but then she knew that Francis, the love of her life was still in there. Maybe buried deep and ever deeper by the day, but he was still there, and that's what kept her going, she would never abandon him.

Mark had taken Francis for a haircut, he'd been attending the same barber down the road for years. Dominick would be understanding of his condition, his mother had died of Alzheimer's a few years back and had lived in with Dominick for a while, but with not sleeping and walking the floors half the night, he'd had to make that awful decision of putting her into a nursing home. He'd said he couldn't continue to give her the care she'd needed and he was beginning to feel the strain himself, she was only a few weeks in the nursing home when she'd died. Dominick was in an awful way, there was no consoling him.

She'd gotten out of her bed in the night and had a fall, never recovered.

Dominick would always make a fuss of Francis; he'd humour him to get the job done. Francis was now finding it hard to sit in one place for too long, so it was a job and a half to get him to sit in the barber's.

As they left, Dominick told Mark to give him a ring next time and he'd call by, to do it at home for him. He'd watched as Mark had struggled to get him into the car.

It's at times like this you know who your friends are, Lizzie had said to Mark when he'd told her, sometimes you have to have the experience of trouble coming to your own door to understand though.

Exhausted after his trip to the barbers, Lizzie knew Francis wouldn't be able to keep his eyes open so she'd left the dinner until later when he'd had a rest, he'd slept for a good hour in front of the TV.

"Hungry?" as she wiped the dribble from his jaw, he'd looked at her, as he raised his hand towards her face it jerked, she'd noticed this before, he touched the side of her face and sort of smiled.

"My darling Francis…I love you…" She took his hand and kissed his head tenderly and he closed his eyes.

Dinner finished, Lizzie decided she would take down the photo album again, he'd enjoyed it last time, she'd left it on his lap and sat down beside him on the sofa. It was a heavy enough album, beautifully designed with lace, covered in plastic on the cover, gold trim all around.

Wouldn't get the likes of it now Lizzie thought and if you did, you'd pay dear for it, she was thinking.

Francis turned the pages and took longer on some pages than others, then he would go back again and look at a page a few pages back before he'd turn to the next. Lizzie watched the expressions on his face, lately she had noticed his face had become expressionless almost. But while he was looking at the photographs, he seemed thoughtful, she'd thought. She wondered what he was thinking, she'd comment on a photograph as he turned the page but she wasn't sure if he'd remembered.

Some she'd hardly remembered herself, they were so old, but some, some brought her back, way back, youth, joy, carefree days.

Where had the years gone? Why was life so cruel? Francis, a man that would do anything for anyone and had worked so hard all of his life. Supported his wife and family without ever a complaint, now battling this soul-destroying disease with all his might so much so that it had left him exhausted, drained of life itself. There were no answers.

There was no doubt in her mind he was fighting a losing battle, but she knew Francis better than anyone, determined, he would battle on as long as his strength would allow him, and then?

Well she wasn't going to think about that now, tomorrow would look after itself, today held enough worries of its own.

Francis stopped on a page of the album that showed a photograph of their twenty-fifth wedding anniversary, for a moment she thought he must remember, excitedly she pointed to her dress.

"Do you remember that awful dress?" Lizzie smiled to herself.

Looking back at Francis she could tell he didn't really remember, he traced the outline of their faces with his finger and just nodded, he looked tired now, enough for today, she thought.

"Let's have a nice cup of tea…eh!" She got up to take the album from Francis but he had a tight hold of it, he could be so strong sometimes. She decided to leave it with him while she put the kettle on, watching from the kitchen, she could see he was watching her as well.

He'd started to tear the pages from the album, not wanting to upset him she had to think about how she would approach this.

"Aw don't tear the lovely photographs…" She picked up the pieces he had torn off and managed to take the album from him without any big fuss. It was like he didn't remember doing it, could only have been five minutes before, but he just looked at her with confusion in his eyes.

"It's okay my love…we can stick them later…no harm done."

Francis was very unsettled that night, would only be in bed when he'd be out of it again, Lizzie had taken him to the bathroom three times, thinking maybe he'd wanted to go there but they'd only have the light on and he'd turn on his heel and walk back to the bedroom again. It had been a long night.

Morning light came with great relief, Francis was sleeping soundly, exhausted after the night. Lizzie thought she would leave him to rest. Do a few bits around the house and get him up later.

Just down the stairs, there was a knock on the door. Jeffrey had noticed the light on in the night and wondered if everything was okay.

"Sure I often see every hour on the clock…be nights and I'm walking the floors myself…was going to knock but didn't want to frighten you."

Lizzie explained how Francis had had a restless night, how she'd left him to sleep for a while, and thanked Jeffrey for his concern.

"Anytime, Lizzie…I mean it…Anytime day or night…don't be on your own…I am always here to help…" Jeffrey was such a good neighbour Lizzie thought, and so concerned. But things would want to be pretty bad before she'd call on anyone that hour of the night.

Tidying up the sitting room, she was reminded of the night before, bits of photographs still on the floor, she would try to tape them together.

Taking the album and the torn bits to the table, she took a quick look upstairs to check if Francis was okay, he was still sleeping.

Some of the bits were badly torn so she just threw them away, taking the photographs that had been torn out of the album as well. She didn't want Francis getting upset when looking at it again, that's if he would remember. It was all very upsetting, looking at one of the photographs that had been torn brought her to tears, it was the one Tim had taken of Francis holding Franie as a very small baby on his lap.

Lizzie remembered it well, a few years ago, now she thought.

Elizabeth had taken ill shortly after Franie was born, Tim had been wonderful, and looked after Franie like it was second nature to him. Would come round in the afternoons then and have a bit of dinner with Lizzie and Francis. Lizzie would send a plate round for Elizabeth to make sure she was eating right. Tim always said she had enjoyed it.

Francis took such pride back then in walking Franie down the road in the pushchair to feed the ducks, sure she'd be asleep by the time they'd got there, but this was his thing to do and continued to do until he wasn't able to anymore. Maybe it had been that little walk every day that had formed the bond between the two of them, there was definitely something special between them, Lizzie always thought.

Mark called in on his way to work, Lizzie had no intentions of telling him about the album, had he not seen it for himself, he'd hugged his mother and went upstairs to see his dad.

"You sit there and finish your tea…I'll get Dad up and dressed…you look exhausted…"

Lizzie put the album away and set the table for Francis to have his breakfast, she might do him a boiled egg today, she'd thought.

There was shouting coming from upstairs, Francis wasn't happy for Mark to dress him. As Mark put on his vest, Francis was taking it off again. He'd taken one of his shoes and thrown it across the room.

"Okay…okay Francis…I'm here…everything's okay…" Lizzie sat on the bed beside him and reassured him everything was going to be alright.

Sitting at the table after his well-earned cup of tea, Mark sighed loudly.

"How do you do it, Mam…it's so hard…maybe we should be thinking of getting some home help in…what do you think…"

Lizzie got up to help Francis with his egg; he was struggling to put the spoon into it.

Chapter 15

"That wasn't a great idea was it…?" She took the spoon and fed him the egg while Mark looked on. "Maybe we'll scramble them next time…" she smiled at Francis and wiped his mouth.

"I know you mean well Mark…and I do appreciate it…but we're fine…"

There was no more about it, Lizzie would relish every moment be it good or bad, this was all she had now and she wasn't going to share it with any home help, no matter how hard it got. She had this.

Mark went into work half-heartedly, he would have to be more hands on, if Lizzie didn't want home help, he would have to be there more, and Elizabeth too. He would talk to her in the evening after work, though in her condition she couldn't be expected to do much, but just to be there itself for support.

Mark had spent every minute of the day dragging by, may as well have been in Timbuktu for all the concentration he'd had. Elizabeth had gone for a lie down when he called on the way home. Soon as Tim got home, she went to lie down, wasn't feeling too good and her back was killing her. "Sure she's carrying Joe around and he's no lightweight at this stage…can't talk to her…anything I can help with…"

Mark pulled out a chair and sat down to talk to Tim, found himself struggling with the words, he was so emotional. There was enough going on in their lives, he'd said, with two young children and another on the way, he would sort something out.

"Maybe I could drop in a bit more…don't like to be intrusive or interfering or anything…I go round with the children often but maybe we could work something out to make it a more regular thing."

"…think your mam would be okay with that…it's no bother to me…could call on the way home of an evening…maybe take Francis for a walk?"

Mark was very appreciative and would mention it to Lizzie, she would surely be delighted.

Elizabeth had heard the chatter and was up and down the stairs in a few minutes, white as a sheet, she'd thought something had happened to her dad when she saw Mark's face.

Going over the whole story again with his sister, Mark found it easier this time to speak, Elizabeth got upset and Tim took Franie and Joe to the swings down the road to give them a bit of space.

"Mam will never tell you that it's getting too much for her…I always ask her…every single time I call…I can see the strain in her face…but it's always the same answer…we're doing fine…" Elizabeth got up to make tea, tears rolling down her face, Mark apologised, upsetting her in her condition was the last thing he'd wanted.

Francis seemed to be getting stiffer by the day, Lizzie thought.

She wondered how long before he wouldn't be able to make the stairs anymore, with no downstairs bedroom she would have to do some reorganising. *Maybe get a sofa bed, that's it,* she'd thought to herself, she would get rid of the sofa in the sitting room and get a sofa bed. Make it a lot easier for Francis.

Delighted with her idea, she rang Mark, she would give him the money to go and buy a sofa bed and ask him to organise the collection of the old sofa by maybe a charity shop or whatever. Maybe he would know someone who would like to have it and wouldn't be insulted by the offer, it wasn't an old sofa and it was very comfortable.

Mark thought it would be nice for Lizzie to go and choose a sofa bed herself, he would organise it for Saturday morning and get Elizabeth to sit with her dad for an hour.

She'd always called round on Saturday mornings anyway, Tim would be there for the day and take the children.

"I was just thinking, Mam…Jeffrey might be interested in the old sofa…I remember when I did a bit of work for him a while back there, he had mentioned the springs had gone on one side of his own one…asked if I could do anything with it."

"…sure I wouldn't know where to start…had a look at it alright…he'd had a board under the cushions where it was going down on one side…"

Mark had picked Lizzie up bright and early to avoid the rush on a Saturday morning, with the market in town, it was always very busy.

"Oh! I don't know Mark…he might be insulted…what?"

Turned out, Jeffrey was delighted with the sofa and the help from Mark on getting rid of the old one, now only fit for the dump.

Francis didn't seem to notice the new sofa bed and sat down without remark. Moving to the sitting room to sleep might be a different story, Lizzie thought to herself. She would have to wait and see, there was time yet, he was still making the stairs albeit with a struggle but still getting there.

"Have you thought about where you'll sleep if Dad moves down here?"

Elizabeth had called by with the children. Franie had noticed the new sofa bed alright, she sat beside Francis as usual, pushing up against him to get closer still. Taking his arm and putting it around her, she was feeling the material with one hand, while sucking her thumb of the other.

"Why is it called a sofa bed Poppy…why not just a sofa like before?"

Looking up at Francis, she moved a bit of his hair that was going across his eye.

"You need a haircut Poppy…when my hair goes in my eyes, mummy always says I need a haircut…"

Francis looked at her without movement and watched as she climbed down from the sofa and into the kitchen to get a biscuit from the jar.

"Just one now young lady…you've had treats already today…"

Elizabeth got up to sit with Francis and Lizzie took them in a cup of tea.

"Dad…how are you feeling today? Do you like the new sofa?"

Nothing, Francis just looked at his daughter as if she was a stranger, heart-breaking.

Lizzie held the cup to give him a sip of tea, she handed him a biscuit, his favourite ones, but he dropped it on his lap, didn't make any effort to pick it up, so she did. His hands were so pale and fragile looking.

Maybe he wasn't hungry she'd thought, but he hadn't had anything to eat since breakfast, he ought to be.

Fr Waters was doing his rounds, called to see if Francis would like to receive Holy Communion, he blessed him and took the Communion out of a little gold box. Lizzie was sure there was a name for this particular box but she didn't know it. Sitting down to pray, Fr Waters held the Communion in front of Francis but he didn't open his mouth. He'd looked over at Lizzie for direction she'd thought, she asked him to maybe half the Communion as he only ate in small portions these days, she was afraid he might choke on it. She took half of it herself and got Francis to take the other half. He chewed on it for the whole time Fr Waters was there, then put his hand to his mouth and took out what was left.

"I'm sorry, Father…maybe another time…he's…"

"Not at all, Lizzie…sure he's grand…" Fr Waters interrupted Lizzie as she spoke, seeing the reaction on her face.

"God Bless ye…you're a great woman, Lizzie…" and he was off.

"It's okay, my love…" Lizzie wiped Francis's mouth as he was still spitting bits of the Communion out of it and she put the TV on.

Francis got up and left the room, as she watched him go, she was hit with the reality of this awful disease all of a sudden. He was getting progressively worse, he looked like a man of ninety today she'd thought, his neck looked so thin from the back and he seemed so stiff as he walked, he stood in the kitchen.

"Is there something you want Francis…?"

"Wha…wha…" He struggled to get a word out.

"Do you want a drink of water?" Lizzie made her way to the fridge to get the jug of water.

No interest in the water, he started to laugh, this was never a good sign. As she left the glass of water on the table, he grabbed her hand, he could squeeze so tight. It was frustration she'd told herself, her Francis would never intentionally hurt her.

Lizzie wondered if maybe Francis would use a walking aid, she remembered working in a geriatric ward as a very young nurse, the sister in the ward was a tyrant, but spotlessly clean. They'd spent any spare time they would have while on duty cleaning and scrubbing in the ward, no such thing as cleaners in those days. It was all a part of the job, to keep your working area spic and span, no fear of infection spreading in those days either. She remembered her hands would be raw from disinfectant in the water, didn't remember wearing gloves back then. It's all so different now she'd thought but she wondered if their methods of cleaning were half as good now as the elbow grease in days gone by.

There were some very challenging moments in that ward, mostly dementia and Alzheimer's patients, she'd just finished training and was delighted to get the job. Some days though she'd regretted not travelling, seeing some of the world while she'd had no responsibilities. But Francis was steadily climbing the ladder in the army and leaving him behind wasn't an option, Francis, even then in the very early stages of their relationship, was her life.

Her first thoughts as she awoke in the morning and her last before she went to sleep at night.

There was a patient that she would never forget, even all these years later, he'd been married for thirty years, she remembered he'd told her, when his wife had died. She too suffered from dementia. Lizzie remembered to this day the tears rolling down his face as he talked about her. She would walk through the ward at night when on night duty and sit with him for a little while, he was always awake when she'd walk by.

His diagnosis was dementia, though in the very early stages but seemed to be progressing quickly. His nephew had concerns about him being on his own when he'd called one day and he seemed very confused. His doctor had admitted him for assessment.

Paddy was his name, a gentler human being Lizzie had never met.

She used to bring him a sneaky cup of tea in the night and maybe a biscuit if there were any leftovers in the staff canteen. He would be so grateful, she would think to herself, for the company more than anything. It must be such a very lonely place to be with no recognition of those around, totally disorientated, and lost.

Paddy became very special to her, the decision had been made that he was not capable of looking after himself at home any longer, so he would be put on a waiting list for the old folks home, attached to the hospital. Which may take a long time, but he would be looked after as an inpatient where he was, until a bed became available for him there.

Chapter 16

How sad, Lizzie had thought, every day she went into work she'd check first to see if Paddy was still on the ward. He remained there for a long time she'd remembered, she couldn't quite remember how long after all these years but she did remember it was long enough to get to know him and get to be very fond of him indeed. It was thinking about getting a walking aid for Francis that put her in mind of Paddy, she remembered the first day he was introduced to the walking aid. He'd been struggling more and more every day to walk up the corridor, she would link him and didn't mind that one bit. But as time went on, she could feel him pulling out of her arm that bit more every day.

He was struggling. She'd organised to get him a walking aid, she remembered it was like getting blood out of a stone, but she got one.

It was like she gave him a pot of gold, he was over the moon.

She would have to tell him to slow down or he'd kill someone and they would have a laugh. It always stuck in her memory, the joy in his face to be able to move around with ease. Of course that too was short lived, wasn't long before his legs had given up and he was confined to a wheelchair.

She wondered how Francis might take to a walking aid, she was beginning to feel the strain in linking him now. Practically his whole weight pulling out of her arm, she would often feel the pain of it in her shoulder, probably strained in every way she'd thought.

Taking off his socks as she got him into bed, still sleeping upstairs, she hadn't introduced him to the sofa bed yet, she noticed one of his socks seemed a bit wet. Having had a closer look she recognised the little pin hole that she'd seen so many times before with an elderly patient, it was the beginning of a leg ulcer.

That was all he needed now, my poor Francis, she'd thought, what next.

Dr Canavan would organise for a district nurse to call and dress Francis's leg a couple of times a week. Mark had insisted on calling the doctor when Lizzie explained what she had discovered on his dad's leg.

"You need this, Mam…you can't do everything for him…you said yourself how nasty these can become if not treated early…"

"I know Mark…it's fine…it's just, you know your dad, how he gets…he's used to me doing things for him…but a stranger…remember how he was when you went up to dress him that day…I don't want him getting upset."

"Sure, we'll see how it goes…might be okay…"

Lizzie dreaded the nurse calling, she knew Francis would too had he any idea, she did try to tell him but wasn't sure he'd taken it in.

Time would tell. Mark was just being helpful, she knew he worried about her as much as his dad did.

Elizabeth had gone into labour; Tim was wondering if he could drop the children off on the way to the hospital.

"I'm sorry, Lizzie…I know it's early…if you could just have them for an hour until I sort something out…"

It was a baby girl, six weeks early. She would have to stay in an incubator for a few days after Elizabeth was discharged, but all was well, a perfect little girl.

Tim had organised a couple of weeks off, for when she was due, but because she was early, he would have to exchange his leave with one of the other lads. His boss, not very understanding of the situation, had wished him luck in finding someone to exchange with.

Paul was only too delighted to help out, "Sure I'm only doing a bit of painting in the house…that can wait…" Tim had thanked him and told him he really appreciated it, Elizabeth would never be able to manage on her own.

Franie up to all sorts and Joe now nearly as mischievous as Franie, they were a handful, not to mention a new born, and Elizabeth still suffering the after effects of a very difficult birth.

"That's it…" she'd assured him afterwards

"No more babies…I'm done."

Francis looked frightened as Elizabeth put baby Lucy in his arms, all the time holding her herself as well, Tim proceeded to take a photograph with Franie. Standing so close to her Poppy, she looked stuck to him and Joe fiddling with his dummy standing in front of Lizzie, Franie doing her best to get up onto her Poppy's knee.

As it turned out, it was a lovely photograph, Francis sitting up as prim and proper as Lizzie had seen him in a while and everybody looking happy.

The nurse would call in the morning. Lizzie talked to Francis as she helped him into bed, he'd been rubbing his leg before he went to bed so she'd thought maybe it was getting itchy, getting better?

That wasn't the case unfortunately, Lisa was a very young district nurse, so friendly and gentle with him. There was no fuss, just a friendly chat that led to a look at the leg.

Lizzie didn't like the look of it at all, what started off only a few days ago like a pinhole, was now a rather large red indent in his leg.

"It's the nature of these unfortunately…Lisa had said…don't worry Francis…you're in good hands…" as she winked at Lizzie.

"I'll make us a cup of tea…" Lizzie left the room and watched from the kitchen to make sure Francis was okay, Lisa was after all a stranger to him and she didn't want him getting upset.

Francis' leg all cleaned up and dressed, Lisa got up to go.

"I won't stay for tea if that's okay, Lizzie…I'm on a very tight schedule today…hope I'm not being rude?"

"Not at all…sure if you leave the dressings, I can dress the leg myself, save you a bit of time…I did nursing for years…well used to it…" Lizzie opened the door for Lisa.

"If you think it's causing him discomfort in any way, I'll leave you a dressing to change it…but if not it's best left for a few days…I'll call in on Friday…thanks, Lizzie…bye Francis, see you soon…"

Lizzie poured the tea and took it into the sitting room to sit with Francis, he had been pulling at the bandage and nearly had it off. He seemed angry, so she just sat with him and gave him his tea, she would deal with the bandage when he'd calmed a bit.

"A nice cup of tea my love…there you are…everything's okay…"

Her heart was broken looking at him, he was having difficulty putting his fingers into the handle of the cup that was new!

Taking a deep breath, she held the cup up to his mouth and he sipped from it. He whispered something in a very low voice but Lizzie didn't catch what he'd said. "What was that Francis?" she put the cup down and took both his hands in hers, he just looked at her.

"Were you saying…I love you…well I love you even more…" He was nodding slowly, she kissed his face and held him for a while.

Franie was kicking up. Tim thought maybe she was a bit jealous of the new baby, he promised her a treat if she behaved and asked her what she would like to do for a treat.

"I want Poppy to take me to feed the ducks…that's my treat…please…please?" She'd been crying and her face looked dirty from wiping her tears after being in the garden.

"You'd better go wash your dirty hands and face then…I'll ring your Nanny and see if it suits…" she was off like a flash.

Lizzie knew the days of Francis taking Franie to feed the ducks had long since passed, she would go with them just to please her.

Tim insisted on walking with them as well. Franie could be a handful and it wouldn't be possible to watch Francis as well, he'd said, and he enjoyed feeding the ducks anyway. They'd laughed.

Lizzie thought to herself how lucky she was, having such a caring family, never one to call on any of them but she knew if need be, they would always be there. She loved to see the children and thought it would break her heart if they'd stopped calling, because Francis was in need of her care twenty-four hours a day, as it was clearly becoming.

She'd always have time for the children no matter what, Elizabeth had asked her only recently if maybe she should leave the small ones at home when she'd call. But she had set her right there and then, although it seemed like Francis didn't take any notice of them at all at times, she knew deep down he was aware that they were around when they were, and that in his own way he would miss them as much as she would if they didn't call.

Children brought life to the place, if only we could be like them, live in the moment, she'd thought, not be wasting our precious days worrying about the days to come. They would come whether we worry or not, and that was one thing for sure.

Climbing the stairs was putting more pressure on Francis's sore leg, Lisa had said in dressing it that day, she'd wondered if there was any way they could set up a bed for him downstairs. His ankles had swollen and would be painful for him to walk, if they got any worse.

Lizzie had dreaded this moment, in all their years in the house, they had both shared their bedroom every single night. Never been apart for a night, except when his work would have him stationed in a different area and that couldn't be helped, and it would only be temporary.

Things were different now though, and changing by the minute.

She'd bought the sofa bed knowing the day would come but she had been holding it off, maybe in denial, she didn't know, maybe just not ready to start this new chapter in their lives, one that could only end in heartbreak.

There were so many others in Francis's life now, they were no longer just him and her like they had been for so long, she didn't like having to share him, not now with every moment precious, it was the beginning of the end.

As Lizzie watched the postman come up the pathway while rinsing her cup at the sink, she was put in mind of the time when Francis was in the army, he would sometimes be given his next station of work by post. She remembered the waiting, hoping he wouldn't have to go too far away. The children were young but it wasn't even that, she would miss him so much when he'd go away. Theirs was a life shared in every meaning of the word, she was lost without him when he had to go.

He would polish his boots every night, she could still smell the polish, then he would go around to the children's bedrooms and take their shoes that they would have worn that day and polish them too, all lined up for the morning, spic and span.

Picking up the post from the hall floor, she tried to recognise the writing, she didn't know why but she'd always done that for as long as she could remember, then finally she would open the letter.

It was from Francis's sister Josephine, always easy-going. She was a very likeable girl, Lizzie was very fond of her.

She wondered if it would be suitable to call for a visit that weekend, she'd been travelling and hadn't been in touch for quite a while. Thought it would be nice to catch up with them all.

Chapter 17

Lizzie wondered if she should fill her in on her brother's condition or would she wait, it was going to be a shock to her to see him so ill and fragile. When she had last visited, they had packed a picnic and gone to the seaside. It was a wonderful day, she was such fun to be around. Lizzie remembered it like it was yesterday, but there had been a lot of water under the bridge since then.

Francis seemed to smile when she'd told him about Josephine's visit, he'd always liked her company, used to say she was mad as a hatter, but she knew he'd had a soft spot for his youngest sister.

Mark would meet her off the train and have a chat with her about his dad, just to put her in the picture, Lizzie didn't think it would be fair not to tell her. She'd been travelling so long with no way of contacting her.

She had given Francis a shower and dressed him in his best shirt and cardigan, he didn't look too bad, she thought to herself.

As she opened the door to them, Mark let Josephine in first.

"Ladies first…" he smiled at his mother.

Josephine had aged too, Lizzie thought, but then she thought to herself, she probably thought the same when she saw her.

She could see she had been crying. "I'm so sorry, Lizzie, for not being in touch…" Lizzie gave her a hug and welcomed her in.

She stood in the kitchen looking in at Francis, who was sitting with his back to her on the sofa, wiped her face and walked towards him.

Mark apologised for having to go but said he would be back later to take her to the train.

"Look at you all dressed up like a toff…" she sat beside him on the sofa and hugged him, eyes closed, tears streamed down her face.

Francis looked up at Lizzie who had walked in behind her, he held his white frail hand on his face and a tear ran down his cheek.

"You know who this is Francis…" Lizzie had to keep herself from getting emotional as well, so she blabbered on explaining how Josephine had been travelling and that had opened up a whole new conversation, the moment had passed. Josephine talked for hours, drank a dozen cups of tea and Francis watched her closely, only turning away when she would catch him watching.

She had seen the world, lonely at times she admitted, but all of her own choice, never one to worry. She was a free soul by nature.

Worn out after the day, Francis had fallen asleep on the sofa.

"I should be on my way…I'm sure you're tired listening to me…"

Josephine got up to go, "Not at all, it was a lovely change." Lizzie offered her another cup of tea.

"Thanks, Lizzie, but my train is in an hour or so…it's been lovely catching up…tough but lovely…" As she kissed her brother on the head, she was off, "Don't leave as long next time…" Lizzie could see she was upset leaving, she would have to deal with this in her own way.

Lizzie remembered how Francis would talk about Josephine years ago, the youngest of the family. She was his favourite sister, always got along well with her. Sounded like she was a bit of a tomboy, Lizzie remembered thinking. Used to play with Francis and his mates, go climbing trees, muck about to her heart's content.

He'd told her they used to play on an old barge when it would rain, many a time his mother would read him the riot act for the state of her clothes when she'd come in. Rust on her hands from the old barge was a real giveaway, he should know better, his mother would say.

Mark had just pulled up outside as Josephine said goodbye at the door

"You and Francis were always, what I would have called soul mates…I remember watching you two dance at your wedding…can still see ye…it was like there was no one else in the room…ye looked so in love…oh! Dear…what can we do, Lizzie…what can we do?"

Josephine closed her coat and continued down the path.

"How's that for timing…" Mark opened the gate for her and closed it after her, winked at his mother and hurried to open the car door for her. No words were spoken, not then at that moment nor at any time on the drive to the station, Mark thought to himself it must have been such a shock for her and left her to her thoughts.

"Thank you, Mark…you're a good lad…goodbye love…"

She stepped onto the train and didn't look back.

Lizzie had made a shepherd's pie for dinner, Francis liked that and it was easy to feed it to him. He'd just about manage a biscuit now with his tea, other than that he needed feeding and watching too, it wasn't so long ago that he had choked on a bit of bread. Lizzie had walked to the kitchen with a cup to put in the sink and had only turned her back for a minute when she'd heard him coughing, he was panicking. She'd reassured him that it was okay, it was only a crumb that had got caught in his throat and he'd be okay. He'd looked so pathetic, so afraid.

She often wondered if her training as a nurse had helped her to cope, she'd watched Josephine fall to pieces, had she just become used to the heartache of looking at her beautiful husband failing before her eyes, or was she bottling it all up and would explode one of the days.

She wasn't sure, she just knew she had to keep going, she couldn't stop to think, it was too hard.

It had been their first Christmas together as husband and wife and Francis had been so excited about putting up the tree.

"We used to have a party around the tree after we'd put it up when we were young…" he'd said.

"…Father would switch on the lights and we'd all cheer…mother would have made a plate of mince pies and we'd sit around the tree for hours…the lights were all colours…I remember feeling so happy and loved…"

Lizzie remembered he'd turned to her and kissed her.

"Are you happy, Lizzie…?"

"Of course I am…why do you ask…?" Lizzie had giggled.

"I want you to be happier than you've ever been…I want you to feel that kind of love that I did back then…I will do everything that I can to make sure of it…I promise you that, Lizzie…I promise you this warm fuzzy feeling will never change…I will love you forever…"

They'd kissed and snuggled under the tree for hours.

She'd gone back years in thought as she watched Francis enjoy his shepherd's pie, wiping the odd dribble.

He'd held his mouth closed tightly half way through the meal.

"Do you have enough Francis…want a drink?"

She'd held the glass up to his mouth but he'd pushed it away. Looking at her in a locked stare, she wondered, "Where are you my love?" She'd wanted to say, "Take me with you?"

She tried with all her might to get him to his feet for bed but he seemed very weak, there was no way he was going to make it up to those stairs tonight, she'd thought. She would let him sleep where he was and get a throw to keep him warm.

Holding him close she whispered to him, "To have and to hold…in sickness and in health…"

Vows taken without a thought of old age and sickness, yet a promise.

To be there no matter what. Old age would have been nice she'd thought, retirement, spending every hour God sent together.

They'd always joked about growing old together, talked of retiring to the sun, strolling along hand in hand without a care in the world. All their life's hard work would have been worth it to sit back in their retirement years and appreciate!

But she knew now that she would neither have nor hold her Francis in their old age.

Lizzie sat up all night keeping the fire going and watching in case Francis wanted to go to the bathroom, or go for a wander.

The night before was to be the last time Francis would get to his feet, at first Lizzie thought he was just tired or his sore leg was keeping him from putting weight on his feet but it was like, overnight he'd forgotten how to walk.

All hands-on deck, the sitting room was transformed into a downstairs bedroom, the sofa bed in a permanent bed position. No longer used as a sofa, it was made to be as comfortable as it could be and all his familiar bits and pieces brought down from his upstairs bedroom.

His medals once shined every day now took pride of place on the mantelpiece where he could look at them. Lizzie was convinced familiarity would keep them from losing him for another little while. Although every day seeming to sink into the fog that little bit more, she would continue to strive to hold on to him.

Elizabeth, finding it all too much, had taken her leave soon as her help was no longer needed.

"I'll call by in the morning, Mam…" she'd had a quiver in her voice as she'd spoken and was off. Mark would stay a while and keep his dad company.

"Mam…" Mark had sat with his dad until he'd fallen asleep, "…what do you think it is that has kept you and Dad so close all these years…you know…I mean, I don't ever remember ye falling out…"

"Oh! Indeed we did…many a time fall out…but never out of love…"

Lizzie seemed to let her thoughts wander, a smile came to her now pale and wrinkled face.

"…You know, Mark…when I first saw your dad…and that's many moons ago now…I knew…I knew I would spend the rest of my life with him."

Mark poured himself a cup of tea, pulled the chair round so that his dad was in view as he sat with his mother at the table.

"…He was a very handsome man in his day…there was something about him…I remember when we were married first and I was on night duty…the money was better if you did the night duty that time…"

"…Your dad would have my porridge warm in the pot when I'd come home and a hot water bottle in the bed for me…oftentimes he would have left for work by the time I got home…"

Mark loved to hear the stories of years ago, stuff he might not have been around to see for himself, or just too young to remember maybe.

He loved to talk with his mother, and dad too when he was able, sadly that time had passed now.

"No cars that time…I would have to get two busses there and two busses back…yes there would be a lovely warm bed to get into after the night…if he'd left before I'd got home then there'd be a note on his pillow…can still see it…"

"Sleep well my darling be home soon…"

A tear came to her eye.

"Mark, it's so hard watching him deteriorate every day…my heart is broken…"

Lizzie got up to go to the bathroom. Mark got up and went to his dad, now sleeping soundly, oblivious to the heartbreak all around him.

The postman came up the garden path as Mark left for home, handing the letter to his mother, Mark gave her a hug and was off.

Sarah, Francis's sister, had received a letter from Josephine, Francis's other sister, to tell her of her recent visit with Francis and how worried she was about their brother.

Chapter 18

"My dear, Lizzie, I am so sorry to hear of dear Francis's illness…I too have been diagnosed with early onset of Alzheimer's disease…very early stages it seems…but nevertheless my dear we all know there is no coming back from the dreaded thing…"

Lizzie was taken aback, was this really hereditary or just plain bad luck. Elizabeth would fret so when she told her, she had already convinced herself it was.

"I do admire you, Lizzie, dear for looking after Francis at home…"

Even in reading her writing you could tell Sarah was inclined to be a bit posh.

"I doubt very much I will have such luxury when I become dependent…as surely I will…can't see my Eric looking after me…I'll be drafted into the nearest nursing home I think…"

This to Lizzie sounded so sad, imagine she'd thought to herself with all their wealth and they were comfortable, she would have no one to look after her at home, surely they could afford round the clock nursing care. At times Lizzie wished she could afford a bit of help, especially at night, the nights were exhausting.

But that was a luxury she couldn't afford, and as for a nursing home!

Not a notion, although a necessity in some cases and there was no doubt in her mind one would get the best of care, she would look after her beautiful husband for as long as she could, it would be her pleasure. And not waste a moment of the precious time they had left together. She only prayed that God would spare her the health to do it.

Sarah went on to say she would call by as soon as she could and if there was anything they needed, anything at all, she had only to write.

She was posh but good-natured as well, when Francis would wake up, Lizzie would read him the letter. She still believed although he seemed lost in his own world, that Francis, her Francis, was still in there, unable to express himself, but maybe he'd still have feelings, she knew he had. She only hoped he'd felt loved and surrounded by those who loved him, as he surely was.

She'd made a nice homemade chicken soup for dinner, Francis would like that, it was one way of getting vegetables into him, she would always say. Never a lover of vegetables and no ambition whatsoever to even taste something new, long as he had a carrot, he was happy. Lizzie would have to hide the onions as she prepared the vegetables for the soup or he'd have a fit, wouldn't tolerate an onion at all, might get away with mixing a parsnip with the carrot occasionally, but not an onion. As she watched him sleep, she thought it was really a shame to wake him but he hadn't eaten in a while and she was beginning to miss him. At that time of day when the children were busy with their own lives, as well they should, it could be very lonely, very lonely indeed.

“Francis…my darling…you must be hungry…” Lizzie sat on the side of the sofa bed and tenderly rubbed her finger across his forehead.

As he awoke, he looked disorientated for a few minutes.

“...it’s okay my love…everything’s okay…look I’ve made us some chicken soup…”

Francis smiled, may have been for other reasons, but Lizzie chose to believe he was happy with the soup. She’d leave a towel on his chest of late to catch the dribbles and always had a face cloth as well to clean his mouth.

When Francis’s nurse came in the morning, she wasn’t at all surprised to see Francis had been moved downstairs.

“That leg would be very sore, Lizzie…apart from anything else…

I will organise a few bits and pieces to make life a bit easier for everybody…have you used the disposable pads with Francis yet?”

Lizzie had been washing three or four times a day, in an effort to keep him comfortable, she’d heard of the disposable pads alright, mind you she’d thought to herself there were no such things in her day nursing.

Seemed degrading at first, but would save a lot of work, she’d been lucky with her training, she knew how to turn a patient in the bed to change sheets and she’d had an old oil sheet from when Mark was young, he’d wet the bed a lot as a child. She was managing for now, but the day would come she’d thought.

“It’s entirely up to yourself, Lizzie, just…it may be better for Francis too…I’m sure you know how hard it is to heal a bedsore…these pads will keep the wet away from the skin…keep him nice and dry…”

Lisa went out to her car to get a few disposable pads, Lizzie had heard of them alright but had never actually seen one before, seemed simple enough to manage.

"Thanks Lisa…I'm sure…" Lizzie all of a sudden got very emotional.

Lisa assured her it wasn't easy and that it was okay to have a good cry.

"Let me show you how it's done…" She explained to Francis every inch of the way and was so gentle with him, all the time making light of the situation. It wasn't at all degrading the way she had introduced it to him. Merely explaining, that because of his restricted movement now, he would be covered in case of accidents, and gave him a big smile and a wink.

Francis co-operated every step of the way. Lizzie hoped it would be as easy for her to do.

When Lisa had left, Francis started to pull at the disposable pad and it ended up on the floor.

She'd spoon-fed him the chicken soup and he seemed to enjoy it. Wiped his mouth and kissed him on the forehead.

"Did you enjoy your soup?" She got up to take the bowl to the kitchen and Francis grabbed her arm. "What is it, my love…?" he struggled to get the words out, but she could tell he was trying to get up and wanted help, he was a ton weight. She could only help him to get comfortable in a sitting position, she wasn't able to lift him.

They'd made a few attempts to stand together, but his legs weren't able to hold him, and neither was she. The walking aid was of no advantage now.

Lisa was around every day now, at first Lizzie wasn't sure that she wanted anybody helping with Francis, but these days she was glad to see her coming.

"I have organised a wheelchair for Francis…might be nice for him to sit outside if the day was nice…what do you think Francis?"

Lisa held his hand as she spoke to both of them, always spoke to Lizzie with Francis, never out of his earshot, Lizzie thought this was so nice. A wheelchair! Would he be able to cope with such a change? Lizzie feared Francis may find this all too much, she would get Mark to be there when it arrived.

Elizabeth thought it was a great idea, "We can take him down to feed the swans…what do you think…" She was talking to Franie who was all ears, though sitting snuggled up to her Poppy in the next room. Elizabeth could see she was tuned in to Lizzie and herself at the kitchen table.

Shrugging her shoulders she put her arm around Francis and looked away. Francis was sleeping.

Wasn't long before Franie had joined him, when it was time to go, Elizabeth had to carry her to the car, no lightweight either, Lizzie thought to herself. Tim had stayed at home with baby Lucy, she'd had a restless night and she was sleeping.

Joe was getting so cute now, watched from his pushchair as his mom carried his sister down the hall to the front door, straining his neck to see round the corner, he'd looked back at Lizzie with his two hands outstretched, palms upwards and said, "Ah gone…"

Lizzie thought this was so cute, she took him out of his pushchair and carried him to the door where he could see everything, his face lit up as Elizabeth came up the pathway.

"My best little man…" She took him in her arms and carried him to the car. Lizzie thought to herself, Elizabeth had her hands full now, what with Lucy a small baby, Joe a toddler and Franie going on twenty!!!

She had such an old head on her shoulders, Franie for a child, Lizzie would always joke with her that she must be going on twenty and she would have a giggle. Not today though, she was out for the count.

Mark pulled up outside the next morning and Lisa pulled up behind him, Lizzie watched through the kitchen window as they took the wheelchair out of Lisa's car. A lump came in her throat, she looked across the hall into the sitting room to where Francis lay, his hands busy picking the fluff off the eiderdown. She missed the old Francis so much, how she longed to talk to him, to explain, to reassure him.

Sure Lisa was so kind in her way with him and Mark would be gentle in explaining to him, as was his way just like his father, but would he understand?

Yet another bit of independence taken away from him. Life was so cruel, so very cruel.

"That was good timing…" Lizzie opened the door with a cheerful smile, she'd hoped they didn't see through it.

Francis had been a great walker in his day, she'd remembered the cold nights well when they were going out together, all she'd want would be to snuggle up on the sofa and watch the burning embers of the fire.

But Francis would have her up and out.

"C'mon lazy bones…let's go take in some fresh air…" He would tease her until she'd got to her feet, she would always give in. Afterwards she would be glad that she had gone. It was so refreshing. Often, she'd struggle to keep up with him, he'd walked so fast, fit as a fiddle. They would hold hands, talk, and talk, always comfortable in each other's company, even the quiet moments felt okay. What was this love that turned adults into children again, playful, happy and carefree, she remembered every moment, and the silly things they used to do. Happy, happy memories.

"What do you think, Dad…want to go for a ride…" Mark wheeled the chair into the sitting room and sat beside his dad on the sofa.

Francis continued to fiddle with the eiderdown.

"Maybe we'll just introduce it today…let you give it the once over…what do you think Francis…?" Lisa winked at Mark and the chair was left beside Francis.

"Cup of tea?" Lizzie had left them to it as she revisited her memories.

"Thanks, Mam…love one…slept in late today, never heard the alarm…twins were organised in ten minutes for school…amazing what you can do when you have to…no time for tea…ate their breakfast in the car…"

Lisa sat at the table. "It's going to take time…then again maybe Francis will take to the chair straight away…some do…some don't…"

She thanked Lizzie for the offer but she would have to have the tea another time, her list of patients was getting longer by the day and no help!

Chapter 19

Elizabeth had a dental appointment and wondered if Lizzie would mind having the children for an hour, she'd been up half the night with a toothache and Tim was working. Lizzie didn't mind, it would be nice for Francis to have the company. She would make some fairy cakes, Franie loved them and Joe would play happily on the mat with his toys, it would be fine.

"Sorry Mam…I know it's a lot to expect with Dad…but I'm miserable…couldn't put up with another night like last night…" Elizabeth looked every bit as miserable as she'd said, her mouth looked a bit swollen Lizzie thought, she'd hoped it wasn't an abscess. She knew from her childhood days that Elizabeth wasn't a fan of the dentist by any means. She remembered taking her once and she'd kicked the dentist, put his tray of instruments flying and screamed her way out of the surgery, and that was before he'd even examined her teeth, he'd only got as far as putting the chair back.

Lizzie had to smile to herself when she'd thought back on the nightmare that Elizabeth had been as a child, one would never think it now with the way she was with her children, she was a wonderful mother.

Baby Lucy was asleep when Elizabeth brought her in from the car, still in her car seat. "She should sleep until I get back, Mam…shouldn't be more than an hour…or thereabouts…thanks…" She gave her mother a kiss and was off on her way. Franie had gone to her Poppy and Joe was already settled into his train set on the mat, it was his favourite spot. Lizzie took the fairy cakes out of the oven and suddenly she was surrounded at the table, as if by a magnet, the lovely smell had drawn the children into the kitchen.

"Will I take one to Poppy…will I…will I…nanny?" impatient as usual, Franie couldn't wait to take the fairy cakes out of the scalding hot tray. She'd burnt her finger in doing so and ran into the room.

Lizzie followed her, she'd often done the same thing herself and it was a sore dose.

"Show me lovey…you poor baby…didn't I tell you they were just out of the oven and they were very hot…come here…let me see…"

Lizzie put some cream on her finger and gave her an extra fairy cake to ease the pain, as if by magic the tears stopped, and with a wipe of her nose on the sleeve of her cardigan, she was fine.

"What's this…?" Lizzie smiled when she'd seen that Franie had put her headphones on Francis's head. "Poppy listening to your music?"

Franie with a mouth full of fairy cake, spluttered that Poppy liked the music. "See Nanny…" she'd pointed at Francis's feet and he was tapping the floor to the music. Lizzie was amazed, maybe, she'd thought, this was something she could do with him. She didn't have headphones but she could get some, she did have loads of old tapes. Maybe he'd remember the music, maybe…she was excited by this.

Mark too was excited to hear there was a reaction to the music, he would get a recorder and headphones and see if the old tapes still played. It was like a miracle, his eyes lit up and he actually started to hum to the music, big band songs from years ago, songs they used to dance to back in the day at the dances and often around the kitchen, if one they'd liked came on the radio. Such happy times.

A simple idea from an innocent child had brought such joy to an otherwise mere existence. She would sit for hours with him holding one side of the headphones to his ear and the other towards her own self and sing along while he'd hum and tap his feet. They had found a way even in the darkest of moments to be close and intimate again.

They would hold hands, his cold and stiffened, hers warm around them.

Time, though borrowed, is ever precious.

Maisie seemed upset on the phone, Lizzie couldn't make out what she was talking about, sounded like something was the matter with Harry, her estranged husband. Hanging up the phone, Lizzie thought to herself, surely she wasn't upset about Harry, sure it had been years since she'd sent him on his way and hadn't she moved on since then with Vincent.

Soon she would know the full story, Maisie had rung to see if it was okay to call by, she'd always ring ahead even though Lizzie had told her often there was no need to be ringing, that she was welcome any time, but she'd ring anyway. Turned out Harry had passed away.

"I'm so sorry Maisie…it was so hard to make out what you were saying on the phone…but I never thought it was that…that's awful news…awful news altogether…"

Lizzie sat her down at the table and put the kettle on.

Should she offer her tea or something stronger, Lizzie thought maybe the tea would be grand, she knew there was a bottle of whiskey in the cupboard somewhere, but she would have to root it out.

Never one for spirits, Francis would enjoy a pint of stout on a night out. Lizzie thought more than likely she'd bought the whiskey for her Christmas cakes at some stage, a good strong cup of tea would be better than any whiskey she'd thought.

"Lizzie, I feel so guilty…maybe if I'd put up with him, he'd still be alive…maybe…oh! I don't know what to think…" poor Maisie was in such a state.

"Now look Maisie…this was nothing to do with you and Harry breaking up…poor soul…God be good to him…those things happen…"

Lizzie told her to drink her tea and that everything would be alright.

"I know he was an alcoholic…and he made my life a misery…for a long time…but you know, Lizzie…I loved him…never stopped loving him…I tried so hard…"

"Shush now…you gave him lots of chances, didn't you? And how many times did he let you down?" Lizzie's words didn't console her friend.

Francis's sisters Dee and Sarah had arranged to call for a visit, Josephine had been in touch and was very concerned about him.

Dee had rung to see if that would be okay, didn't want to cause any inconvenience, so they would call at a time that suited Lizzie.

Lizzie was only too delighted to see them call, it had been too long.

"My dear, Lizzie…how are you at all…and poor Francis how is he…?" Ever the drama queen, Sarah had her handkerchief out as Lizzie answered the door.

Dee trailing behind, making faces at her behind her back.

"Hello, Lizzie…lovely to see you…" Lizzie had to smile.

"…however bad you were…prepare to be a lot worse after the mother of sorrows herself…she'd put years on a donkey…" Dee was so funny.

"And you know, Lizzie…I was telling you wasn't I…I'm in the very early stages myself…" Sarah had her little mirror out to fix her lipstick.

"Sure we're all doomed…" Dee made her way into the sitting room.

"Francis my good man…isn't it well you're looking…and you all cosy and comfortable there…" Dee gave her brother a hug and moved aside to let Sarah, who was practically on her heels in around her.

"Aw poor Francis…how are you my poor dear…isn't it dreadful…and—" Dee interrupted Sarah, knowing what was coming next. She wasn't sure if Francis would take it in, but he didn't need to know the whole family seemed to be cursed with the darn thing, he'd had enough to deal with. Not one for doctors, Dee would prefer to remain ignorant, "Nothing they can do about it anyway, far as I can see…tell me, Lizzie, how are all the babies…keep you busy I bet…"

Lizzie had prepared sandwiches and made a tea break. They watched as she put the towel over Francis's chest and fed him a piece of tea break. Lovingly wiping the crumbs from his mouth after. Dee smiled at her with sadness written all over her face.

Elizabeth arrived with Franie just as the ladies got up to go.

Lizzie was worried Sarah would mention her diagnosis, she hadn't discussed it with Elizabeth, she knew she would worry too much and she'd had enough to be thinking about for the moment. There was no mention of it, Lizzie breathed easy once they had left.

"Didn't Auntie Sarah get older looking…do you think?" Elizabeth watched them drive off from the window

"What did they think of Dad?"

Lizzie wondered if perhaps this was a good time to tell her of her aunt's diagnosis, maybe not, maybe tomorrow.

Harry's funeral was arranged and Maisie wondered if Lizzie might like to accompany her.

"Vincent is out of town…and anyway I'm not sure if it would be the right thing to do…to go to your ex-husband's funeral with another man in tow…what do you think, Lizzie?"

Lizzie knew by Maisie's voice that she needed her support and she assured her she would be there for her. Mark would be only too willing to step in and look after his dad, Elizabeth was a different story, it would mean her organising someone to look after Lucy for the few hours, it was much easier to ask Mark. With Francis the way he was, he needed the full attention of whoever was looking after him, looking after a baby as well was out of the question. Things were moving on now at a steady pace, looking back only a few months previous, things had certainly moved on and not in a good way.

Francis had begun to pull his hair out, Lizzie had often wished she'd had the head of curls he'd had in his young days, she used to say it was wasted on a man .He'd have it cut as soon as it started to curl, even now he still had a good head of hair, though white as snow.

She would watch him as he twirled it round his finger now and pull bits out every time. It was heart wrenching to watch.

Maisie was taking Harry's death very badly, she seemed full of regrets.

"I should have tried harder, Lizzie…I knew he had a weakness for the drink the day I married him…why could I not have dealt with it after we married…? I loved him the same…what changes with marriage?" She had sobbed all the way to the graveyard, Lizzie had never seen such a sad funeral, the chapel barely half full, and it was a small chapel. She wondered where all of his drinking buddies were, he always seemed so popular.

As if reading her thoughts, Maisie looked around the graveyard and wiped her eyes. "When he had money for a drink, he had plenty of friends." She threw a red rose in on top of his coffin and walked away.

Mark had made the tea when Lizzie returned.

"Thought Maisie would be back for a cup of tea…"

He was surprised to see his mother on her own.

Lizzie explained she'd had a headache; she'd asked her back alright but she'd said all she wanted to do was to lie down.

"She's taking Harry's death very badly…she was so upset…I'll give her a ring later to see if she'll come round for a chat maybe…"

Francis had tried to get out of the bed and fallen, Mark had gone to the bathroom. "I was two minutes I'd say Mam…that was all…"

He was fine. Lizzie put the music on and held the headphones in place, one at Francis's ear and the other at her own and sat with him for hours, ended up nodding off together.

Chapter 20

The room was dark when she woke up, she moved very quietly so as not to wake Francis, seemed so much like his old self when he was sleeping. Time meant nothing now, no such thing as sleeping at night and awake in the day, these days you slept when you could.

Elizabeth had been up all night with Lucy

"Saw every hour on the clock." She'd yawned all through her words.

"…I know you don't get much sleep, Mam…don't know how you do it…I am wrecked…" She glanced down at Lucy who was sleeping in her pram. "…well for some eh!"

Lizzie put the kettle on. "Why don't you go up and lie down for an hour? I'll watch Lucy…sure isn't she grand there sleeping away…go on…"

Elizabeth went into the sitting room to say hello to her dad but he was sleeping, so she went off up to bed for an hour.

Lucy had slept for most of the morning and so did Elizabeth.

The doorbell rang and woke Lucy who didn't know where she was after waking out of her sleep, she had started to cry, all she wanted was her mum.

Elizabeth came running down the stairs

"Sorry Mam…I just hit the pillow and I was gone…c'mere sweetheart…" She lifted Lucy out of her pram and cradled her in her arms. She had fallen back to sleep again within minutes, still exhausted after the sleepless night.

"Dad awake?" Elizabeth peeped into the sitting room not wanting to disturb him, rocking Lucy in her arms as she went.

"…he's sleeping a lot, Mam, isn't he…?"

Lizzie smiled at the concern in her daughter's face and reassured her he was catching up too after a very agitated night.

"Seems to settle better during the day…gets anxious in the night sometimes…"

"…God Mam…it must be the most awful feeling…wonder if he's…oh! It's just so awful…I think I would rather be dead…sorry Mam…"

Elizabeth had tears in her eyes as she tucked Lucy into her pram.

Her words went round in Lizzie's head.

"I think I would rather be dead…" Lizzie wondered, given the choice, would Francis rather be dead? It was such an awful existence. Was she being selfish holding on to the hope that he would see another year, another month, another day?

All she knew was that she could still hold his hand at night and sit with him to listen to music, she didn't care what people said, she knew in her heart that Francis still knew her. It was this fog…this awful fog that was blocking everything out. She would hold on to hope and take one day at a time. She would make a nice cup of tea and maybe read to him for a while, it had been a long time since she'd sat down to read. She could still see Francis with his glasses half way down his nose, doing the crosswords on the Sunday paper, she'd be pottering around the kitchen seeing to the Sunday lunch. Could almost feel the contentment even now just looking back. Being together, whatever, wherever, it was all they'd wanted in life, never wanted what anyone else down the road had, never wished for what they couldn't afford. Their needs were very basic, worked hard for what they had, and relished every moment shared.

Lizzie read aloud while Francis seemed to listen, every now and then he would raise his hand to his face, as if to say something.

"You okay my love..." she had come to know the signs, whatever it was he wanted to say, she assured him everything was okay. He'd nodded his head and whispered yes in a very low voice, and she'd taken his frail hand in hers, it was cold as ice even with a blanket round him and a fire blazing in the room.

Continuing to read, Lizzie found she couldn't get the words out, she was choking with emotion, she wanted to cry out, though she'd tried so hard not to, she'd cried in his face.

"My beautiful Francis...my beautiful darling..."

She had never felt so alone.

"Mam...you okay...?" Mark had come into the room and Lizzie had never heard him coming, still sobbing, she was so disappointed in herself for letting him see her in such a state. She was supposed to be the strong one, the one that was coping so well. Mark knelt down in front of his mother and father, who'd drifted into a sleep by now and he sighed. "...I thought...Mam you gave me a fright...I thought..."

He hugged his mother and they cried together.

"Aren't we a right pair eh...we'll let him sleep...have a nice cup of tea..." Lizzie got up to go to the kitchen and put

Francis's cold hands inside the blanket, and kissed his forehead.

Mark wiped his eyes and followed her in, passing her out in the hallway to go to the bathroom. *We are none of us strong in the face of sickness,* Lizzie thought to herself, but she must not let her guard down again like that.

What if it had been Elizabeth with the children, to see their Nanny in such a state, no she would have to hold her emotions. Even a heart that's broken still beats, she would soldier on.

Mark had always had time to chat, Lizzie appreciated that. Elizabeth was busy with her young family but even when she was around, most conversations revolved around herself and the children, that was life Lizzie thought, she chatted to Mark for nearly an hour before the doorbell rang. Elizabeth, all flustered came through the door like a hurricane, "Joe…he's fallen in the playground…can you take Franie, Mam…have to take him to the doctor…hit his head and he looks awful pale…" Lizzie reassured her that he would be okay, but it was always safer to have that sort of thing checked out.

"Best be on the safe side…go on, I'll look after Franie…" Lizzie took Franie by the hand and closed the car door behind her.

"What about Lucy…where's Lucy?" Elizabeth pointed through the car window to Lucy fast asleep in the back, anxious to get going she'd tried to smile, "She'll be okay…I'll manage her…"

While looking in at Lucy, Lizzie could see Joe sitting very still and pale as a little ghost, there were no signs of a fall that she could see, but he did look pale.

"Can I sit with Poppy…" Franie oblivious to what was going on was skipping along up the pathway.

"Ignorance is bliss," Lizzie said to herself.

"Of course you can lovey…but wait until you see who's in here."

Lizzie opened the front door and Franie ran into the kitchen.

"Uncle Mark…our Joe fell off the swing…can I sit with Poppy…?"

Before Mark could answer, Franie had already ran into the sitting room, and was snuggled up beside Francis when he followed her in.

He watched as she took her grandfather's hand and wrapped it around her. He wasn't sure if his dad was even aware that she was there, but that wasn't stopping her. She was ranting on about how Joe had fallen off the swing and at the same time rubbing her Poppy's ear.

Lizzie sat on the other side of Francis to give him his snack, he loved a biscuit with his cup of tea.

"Nanny…" Lizzie didn't know what was coming next.

"Why is Poppy's hands so cold…why doesn't he talk to me anymore…mummy said he's just a bit tired…is he just a bit tired?"

Lizzie smiled at the innocence on her little face.

"Yes lovey, Poppy is a bit tired…" normally she would have corrected her and told her she should say "why are" and not "why is," but today she didn't have the heart.

"…and mummy said if Poppy gets weally weally tired, he will have to go for a big big sleep…like when I had a sore tooth and I didn't sleep…I had to go for a big big sleep too…" Lizzie fought to keep back the tears.

Turning to her grandfather, Franie stopped rubbing his ear and rubbed his face instead

"Don't worry Poppy…you have a nice big sleep and I'll be here when you wake up…shh…" She climbed down from the sofa and on her tippy toes, she left the room.

Mark took her in his arms and brought her into the kitchen to the biscuit jar. "Let's see if Seanie and Alfie have left you any biscuits…"

Turned out Joe was fine, more shocked than anything, got an awful fright, the poor devil, he would be fine just to keep an eye on him.

Francis enjoyed his tea and biscuits. Lizzie dunked the biscuit into the tea to make it nice and soft for him, often she would leave it too long in the tea and end up leaving half of it behind.

She thought of how Elizabeth had said it to Franie about her grandfather going for a big sleep, was she preparing her for the worst, maybe, and what a lovely gentle way of explaining it to a child.

Lizzie hoped that day would never come, she didn't know how she herself would deal with it, let alone a child. She didn't like to think about it, tomorrow would look after itself, today had enough worries of its own.

Maisie sounded very weak on the phone, she'd come down with the flu a few days after the funeral and had been bed ridden for a week.

"Why didn't you let me know you were laid up…you're a devil…" Lizzie was feeling bad because she hadn't contacted her in a couple of weeks, but she thought maybe she needed the time on her own, and there was Vincent, didn't seem to be talking much about Vincent these last few times they'd spoken.

"I'll call round soon as Mark comes this evening…"

Maisie wouldn't hear of it, what if Lizzie was to pick up the flu and all that depended on her, no she would be fine and she wasn't to come within a mile of her.

Soon as Mark called in as he always did after work, Lizzie made her way to the shop and packed all the essentials she could think of into a box and sent Mark round to Maisie's on his way home. He would leave them on the porch for her so that she wouldn't be cross or worried that he might pick up the flu. Hanging up the phone, Lizzie's heart went out to her friend, with all the ups and downs, and goodness knew they'd had plenty, she wouldn't change a minute of having a family, it was such a blessing. Being on your own must be the saddest thing, she'd thought, especially if you weren't well.

Francis seemed brighter that day, appeared to be looking around, taking an interest even, Lizzie chatted to him as usual as she pottered around the room. The nurse was due any minute and he was going to have a bed bath, there was a time that she could manage herself, would have it done by the time the nurse called. Thought it was degrading enough having your wife wash you down beside a complete stranger, but these days she just thought needs must. This was such a degrading disease, stealing every bit of dignity along with every bit of independence, bit by bit, every single day. It would never steal his gentle soul, Lizzie knew that nothing could steal that away.

"Isn't that nice and fresh now Francis…?" as the nurse dried his chest area, Francis grabbed the towel and jerked it from her, he threw it across the room. Lizzie had just come through the door with a tray of tea and biscuits, well deserved by all, she'd thought as she went to put the kettle on.

Chapter 21

"My goodness…Francis, it's okay…I'm here now…it's okay…"

Leaving the tray aside, she pulled the blanket over him and held him, he was shivering, she should have stayed and helped, usually once he was washed, the nurse who is always so good with him would have him dressed in no time, but not today.

All powdered and puffed, he was dressed and warm, and settled again in no time

"I'm so sorry about that…" Lizzie wiped the sweat from her brow.

"All a part of the territory I'm afraid, Lizzie…as I'm sure you know well…good days and bad…unfortunately at this stage, more bad than good…." She packed her bag and was off. No time for tea that day, she was covering for another nurse in the area as well that week.

Sitting with Francis, having a cup of tea, Lizzie thought back to the days after they'd first met, how she'd be watching the clock to finish her shift, so that they could be together again. There was never enough time, she'd always want more and so it was to this day, she still wanted more. She watched as he curled the end of the quilt round and round on his finger, it seemed to bring him comfort.

"Are you okay my darling…can I get you anything…?" if only!

"Hi, Lizzie…said I'd give you a ring while I can still remember your number dear…" Sarah sounded well, though diagnosed with Alzheimer's, was showing no signs as yet, still independent and hoped to remain that way for a long time yet.

"How's dear Francis doing…? I keep meaning to call over but the weather has been so miserable…I just run to the shop and straight home again…I do think of the two of you though…every day…"

There was a bit of kindness there, Lizzie thought, just a small bit. Francis always said Sarah only ever worried about Sarah, but at least she'd rang and was thinking of them.

Jeffrey always called in on a Monday afternoon.

"Off with you now, Lizzie, and have a little break for yourself…myself and Francis will be grand…isn't that right young fella…?"

He'd sit himself down beside Francis and chatted away to him, more often than not, Francis would nod off, but Jeffrey wouldn't mind.

Lizzie had her few bits written down for the shopping, her head was all over the place this weather, she would go to the shop for something in particular and meet someone and it would be gone out of her head. Often come home without the one thing she went out for.

A list was the best thing she'd thought, she didn't want much, just a few things. Thought she might bake a few fairy cakes, Elizabeth was calling round later with the children and they loved the fairy cakes.

Make them for half the price you'd pay for them in the shop too, and so much nicer when they're made at home. These days Lizzie found a bit of baking sort of therapeutic, relaxing.

Francis spent so much time now sleeping, she had a lot of time on her hands, and had to keep busy, otherwise she would be doing too much thinking.

"I'm sorry Jeffrey…got caught talking to Mrs Geary coming up the hill…sure she'd talk the birds down from the trees…is everything okay…?"

"Sure yer grand…there's no hurry in the world, Lizzie…where am I going? We had a lovely chat…didn't we Francis…? I think the pair of us had a little snooze as well…"

They had a laugh. Lizzie made a cup of tea and Jeffrey was still there when Elizabeth called with the children, no fairy cakes today!

Lucy was teething and very cranky with it, Franie went straight into her Poppy and sat down beside him, taking his arm as usual and putting it around her.

"That Lucy is so annoying Poppy…she's crying and crying…gives me a headache…" she snuggled up to Francis and was asleep within minutes. Elizabeth was looking worn out too, Joe played away with his toy tractor on the floor, happy as Larry.

"No sleep in our house last night…" Elizabeth held Lucy on her lap until she finally nodded off.

Francis refused to eat his dinner, it was the first time ever. Lizzie had mashed some potatoes with broccoli, just the way he liked it. Of late she wasn't able to give him meat, he used to gag on it so he was sort of vegetarian these days. But today he wasn't opening his mouth and pushed her hand away.

"Okay love…maybe later eh! We'll leave it till later…" Lizzie held back the tears, it was just heart-breaking. She would try him with some ice cream later, he loved ice cream.

Mark thought he'd seen a change in his dad overnight.

"Did he sleep last night, Mam? He looks…I don't know…out of it a bit…"

This scared Lizzie, she'd seen this before in working with patients with Alzheimer's, there was no doubt his condition was progressing, and faster than she had hoped.

"Oh…you know…the usual…never sleeps the night…" She looked in at her husband, the light fading now, throwing shadows across the room.

She hated the nights with a passion, it was so, so lonely, she loved to see the daylight coming, didn't matter if she hadn't had any sleep the night before, it would give her new energy.

"Now Francis…I know it's not very appropriate to be eating ice cream for supper…but just this once…" Lizzie held the spoon of ice cream to his mouth but he didn't open it.

He hadn't eaten a thing all day, she hadn't said anything to Mark, he'd only worry. She dipped her finger into the bowl of ice cream and put it to his mouth. It took a minute, but he opened his mouth and licked the ice cream.

"Isn't that nice…?" He sort of smiled at her and put his hand to his face as if to wipe his mouth. His hands were now white as snow, fingers together as though they were webbed.

All tucked up for bed, Lizzie stretched out on the armchair beside him, Francis, the Francis she knew and loved, was almost gone now. Still convinced he was in there somewhere, trying to get out, Lizzie would strive to hold on to that thought, it was keeping her from going insane.

Awoken by the ring of the doorbell, Lizzie got up with a start, she must have slept the whole night through, in her clothes. As she passed by Francis, she touched his face, she would always do that, was it checking to see if he was still with her or just a show of affection, she wasn't sure. The nurse was surprised to see the curtains closed when she came up the path, she'd said, was hoping everything was okay.

"This is Ita, Lizzie…she will be covering my holidays for the next couple of weeks…"

Lizzie shook her hand and the nurse showed her into the living room.

"…and this is Francis…"

Barely awake Francis just looked scared.

"Francis…this is Ita…she will be looking after you for a couple of weeks while I'm on holidays…"

"A well-earned break…" Lizzie opened the window to let a bit of fresh air into the room after the night.

She went to put the kettle on and left the ladies to their work, she felt exhausted, normally she would be in there helping out, but today she was happy to let them get on with it. There was enough in two, she would only be in the way anyway.

Ita seemed very quiet, maybe it was just her way, Lizzie wasn't sure. She sat without a word while they had a quick cup of tea.

Mark came up the path as they drove off. "New nurse?"

Francis wasn't at all impressed, was kicking off the bedclothes and shouting out all morning. There would be no work done today, Lizzie thought, what harm the work can wait.

Turned out Ita had recently lost her dad, he had suffered from Alzheimer's, lasting seven years. She had seen a lot of her dad in Francis and found it upsetting.

"I am so sorry, Lizzie…I know it must seem very unprofessional of me…but it's like they have the same…oh I don't know…that lost look in their eyes…you know…it's such a horrid…horrid disease…"

Lizzie sympathised with her and told her of her own days working on a geriatric ward, and how, though it was staring her in the face, she just couldn't bring herself to accept that Francis was so ill.

She just wasn't ready to accept that yet, not yet.

Francis's sister Dee arrived on the doorstep.

"I suppose I should have told you I might call…" she shuffled her way down the hall into the kitchen, "…but you know, Lizzie, you make plans and something always turns up…and then there's disappointment…better to surprise than disappoint I always say…" dropping her bag on the floor beside her, she plonked down on the chair at the kitchen table.

"My poor feet…how are ye all anyway?"

Lizzie smiled as she filled the kettle.

"We're okay now Dee…how are you and Bartley doing?"

"Bartley!!!…sure what would be wrong with any man…dinner served up to them…house cleaned…long johns washed…what more could they want…it's a man's world, Lizzie…and no two ways about it…I'll have the cuppa and I'll go in to see Francis then…how's he doing, the poor soul?"

"Good days and bad now Dee…good days and bad…but we still have him…that's what matters, isn't it?"

“Goodness…that’s a lovely cup of tea…can always depend on getting a nice cup of tea here…I have a friend I go to visit every now and then…jeepers, you could trot a mouse on the tea, it’s so strong…there’s strong and there’s strong…”

Francis didn’t seem to want his cup of tea that day.

“He’s not eating as good as he used to Dee…it worries me a bit…”

“He’ll be eating enough…he isn’t going to run a marathon, is he…? Don’t be worrying…sure a small bit would do when you’re not active…you’re only bringing bother on yourself stuffing him…you know what I mean…” pointing at the commode in the corner of the room, Dee winked at Lizzie.

“Dee you’re terrible…wouldn’t bother me if I had to change him ten times a day…stop you’re desperate…” and they had a giggle.

The commode was only an ornament in the corner of the room, used but a couple of times when Francis was aware that he needed it, now he had lost all of that awareness, he was as dependent now as a new born baby. Dee’s visit as usual was like a tonic to Lizzie, she was so funny and witty. She’d hidden her heartbreak in looking at her brother so ill, but Lizzie knew inside, behind the witty comments and cheerful way, she too was broken. Lizzie took down the photo album when Dee had left, Francis turned the pages quickly as if looking for a particular photo, Lizzie wondered what, if anything he was looking for.

She helped him to turn the pages more quickly to see if he might stop at a specific page, but no, when they got to the end of the album, he was looking for more pages to turn.

Chapter 22

What was going on inside his head? What torment? She just wanted to hold him and protect him from the world. Holding him, as she did sometimes well into the night, she could feel his bones, his skin only holding them together, his flesh now melting away before her eyes.

"My precious Francis." she would whisper into his ear every morning and every night, she believed he knew who was talking to him, he knew he was so loved.

Franie came through the door like a hurricane, totally ignored Lizzie who was standing at the sink, went right into the sitting room to Francis. As Lizzie dried her hands, she could see Elizabeth struggling with taking the buggie from the boot of the car, Joe still in his car seat crying, and baby Lucy asleep in the front car seat. It's not easy, she'd thought to herself and even harder when you're carrying a heavy heart.

Elizabeth had rang her the night before to see if it was okay to call over in the morning, "I know it's a bit much, Mam, with Dad the way he is…but Franie is on and on about her Poppy…wanting to come over…"

Elizabeth had got upset on the phone.

"What is it, Elizabeth…what's the matter…of course it's okay to bring the children round…sure we love to see them…why are you upset?"

Lizzie could hear the sobbing at the other end of the phone.

"I'm so worried about Dad…Mam…do you think he's failed a bit lately…? It's tearing me apart looking at him…I don't think…"

"Shush…now…look, come over in the morning for a nice cup of tea."

Lizzie knew full well that Francis was indeed failing, she would make the most of things, no sense going before God.

"Well Missy, where did you come from?" Lizzie went in to see Franie in the room, snuggled up as usual beside her Poppy, one headphone on her ear and holding the other to Francis's ear.

"Poppy loves my music…I picked it especially for him…see…" Franie pointed to her Poppy's hand that seemed to be tapping on his lap.

"Yes love…he loves music…especially your music…" Lizzie wished she could once again feel the innocence of a child, just for a little while. It wasn't long before both Franie and her Poppy were fast asleep.

Joe had stopped crying the minute he was released from the car seat and running up the path, it was like his mother had turned off a switch.

A quick hug for his Nanny and a beeline for the biscuit tin.

Lucy was still sleeping, "Wish she'd sleep at night!"

Elizabeth left the buggy in the hallway and went in to see her dad, who was sleeping.

"Bad night?" she flopped down on the chair at the kitchen table and thanked her mother for the tea.

"Aw sure…same as usual…just have to go with it…didn't give him his breakfast yet now…just tidied him up and made him comfortable…"

Elizabeth had seen a change in her dad in the last few visits.

"I don't know Mam…is it his colour or just the way he looks at you…it's like…he's crying out to you…but you don't know how to fix it."

"Here…have a biscuit…" Lizzie didn't want her getting upset, Joe was watching her very closely.

"…you look tired…are you sleeping?"

"I'm okay Mam…it's just so frustrating…you know…he's my dad…"

Elizabeth picked Joe off the floor where he was playing with a little car he'd brought with him, she cuddled him, "…he's my dad…"

For a moment there was quiet, Lizzie hated the quiet.

Franie came into the kitchen. "Did you wake up…?" Elizabeth pulled the chair beside her out, from under the table and she sat on it.

"Want a bikie?" She handed her a biscuit from the tin and she shyly took it, Elizabeth winked at her mother. "What do you say?"

"When will poppy be all better…I want to show him the ducks…he didn't see them for a long long time…and he looks so sad…I think he's missing them…"

Sticking her finger into the jam on the biscuit, she put it into her mouth.

Elizabeth left Joe down onto the floor again and went to the bathroom.

Jeffrey had come in to the back garden to take the bins out, he was such a good neighbour. Lizzie could be sure he would be out first thing to bring them in the next day. He'd tap on the door then to see if everything was okay, he hadn't been such a regular visitor as he used to be. Lizzie reckoned he probably didn't want to be in the way with all the comings and goings these days, so she would always call him in for a cup of tea.

"How are you young fella…" He would sit with Francis to have his tea, never remark on how he'd look or how his mood had been, he could sit with him for an hour without saying anything, just for the company.

Lizzie thought to herself, he probably feels lonely himself too sometimes, living on your own could be lonely. Although she had Francis, sometimes she'd feel alone too, especially in the night.

Mark would come round to give his dad a shave, these days once a week would suffice. Francis seemed to enjoy it, he'd raise his chin and watch every movement as Mark cleaned the razor, he'd always said the wet shave did a better job. Francis had taken to the electric shaver shortly before he'd got laid up, but Mark had no confidence in them either.

"Was thinking Mam…might go for a walk, take Dad in his chair…what do you think…it's a lovely day?"

It took a bit of effort but they got him into the chair, Lizzie walked by his side to watch his feet, although there were footrests on the chair, his feet would slide off them, he wouldn't realize it.

It was a lovely break from the house for him, Lizzie had thought.

"What do you think, Dad…will we do it again…?" Mark was delighted with himself, he would certainly do it again and make the most of the fine weather.

As they lifted him out of the chair, Francis took Mark's wrist and squeezed it very tightly.

"Okay, Dad…let go of my wrist now…c'mon Dad…"

There was no letting go, Mark, as much as he hated doing it, had to prise his father's hand from his wrist, it was all marked.

"…you have some grip there…" As he continued to lift his dad onto the sofa, taking most of the weight from his mother, Mark could see the cross look in his eyes. He would be worn out now after that episode. It would have taken him all of his strength to grip his wrist like that, pure frustration, Mark thought to himself, and why wouldn't he be frustrated. His wife changing his nappy, his son deciding when he could go out, his legs no longer able to support him. Frustration wasn't the word, this was pure torture for a man so capable, so gentle, so private, pure torture!

Lizzie would run to the shop now that Mark was there, pick up a few bits. It was so handy that the shop was but a few minutes away, she missed her trips into town though, into the big shops, the fashion, the chat with people she'd meet. Often in days gone by, she'd thought to herself, Francis would accompany her into town, maybe at birthdays and that. Get her to pick a nice outfit or treat her to a bottle of perfume, he was decent when he'd have a few bob, always liked to share it with her and buy her something. She missed the old Francis so much, the one that would sneak up behind her while she'd be cooking and steal a kiss or turn up the volume on the radio and ask her to dance in the middle of peeling the potatoes, such memories, such lovely memories.

Wondering what to get for the dinner, she was away in a world of her own when she got a tap on her shoulder.

"Fr Waters…didn't even see you there…"

"Lizzie, how are you…I was meaning to call to see Francis…it's so hard to get to everybody…how is he, the poor man? There's such a lot of sickness around…" Fr Waters went on to talk nonstop for twenty minutes or so, Lizzie just listened.

Kitty had arrived with the twins when Lizzie got home, Eilish had gone to a birthday party. The boys weren't a bit impressed that they weren't invited, so Kitty promised them they would go to see Nanny and Poppy after school.

"Nanny…what would you say to this young boy who pulled a little girl's hair in school today?" Kitty winked at Lizzie.

"My goodness…I'm shocked…surely not Alfie?"

Alfie, with his mouth full of biscuit, dribbled all over his shirt as he spoke.

"Not me Nanny…not me…it was Seanie…he's always getting into trouble on the yard…"

Seanie had a face on him as long as a wet week and without even looking up, he retaliated

"Not true…I was only playing…she pulled my shirt first…anyway it was just her pigtail…" he got down from the table and went into the sitting room.

Mark smiled to himself and looked at Kitty.

Lizzie couldn't wait to get her feet up after they'd left, it was so lovely to have them round, tantrums and all.

Sitting beside Francis who'd had a fairly good day, apart from the episode of getting him out of the chair earlier, she kicked her shoes off and took his hand in hers. It was cold as ice, she cupped it in both her hands until it felt almost warm again. She snuggled up to him and just enjoyed the quiet, it didn't take her long to nod off. When she awoke, the place was in darkness and Francis was awake.

"I think I might have dropped off…" she got up to turn on a light but he had a grip on her hand. She would wait a while, a tear rolled down his cheek and she wondered what he was thinking, he looked so sad, it was heart wrenching.

Gently, she removed his hand from hers, while talking to him about meeting Fr Waters at the shop and how there were so many people ill in the community. Maybe he understood what she was saying, she wasn't sure, but he was looking at her and seemed to look concerned, then again, maybe not.

Pottering around the kitchen, Lizzie gave the odd glance into the sitting room, Francis was twirling the blanket round his finger and had his eyes closed. "A bit of rice pudding…that's what I'll make for tea…"

Francis loved his puddings. She put a towel under his chin and fed him with a small spoon. "Is that nice?" she waited for him to finish a spoon before she offered the next one. He seemed to chew and chew while looking around the room, that would take a while but at least he didn't turn it down. Lately he would close his lips tight if he didn't want to eat, and there was no coaxing him, she did worry that he wasn't getting enough nourishment.

Elizabeth was concerned about her mother, she thought she was looking very tired, she would talk to Mark about maybe organising a bit of home help. Mark had mentioned this before to Lizzie but things had become a lot more difficult since then, he would ask her again.

"What do you think, Mam…maybe a night nurse so that you can get a bit of sleep even…" He could see his mother was feeling a bit defeated. "…there's no shame in asking for a bit of help, Mam…I know you're doing a great job with Dad…but we worry that you're here on your own at night…do it for our peace of mind…will you?"

A night nurse was organised and Lizzie didn't argue the point this time.

Chapter 23

Mind you, it was made perfectly clear that she would only come when called upon, Lizzie would look after Francis, but it would indeed be good to have a bit of help in changing him if he needed it through the night, which he so often did.

Not to mention the company, it would be nice to have the company.

Mark had seen every hour on the clock right through the night, it was the first night that the nurse would stay with his dad, he wondered if they'd done the right thing in talking his mother into getting a bit of help at night. Was it for their own peace of mind or for their mother's? He wasn't sure, all he knew was that he'd hated leaving her on her own with him, especially in the evenings when the night could be so long.

What if his dad had got difficult in the night, he could be very strong in one of his angry moments, as his mother used to call them.

"That's not Francis," she would say. "It's this dreadful disease…"

He was glad to hear the alarm go off in the morning, must have fallen asleep just before it went off, exhausted after twisting and turning all night long. If only our minds could switch off for a while, he'd thought, they could be a torment at times, and usually in the night!!!

Turned out his night of anguish was in vain, his dad had had a very peaceful night, slept through.

"You look like a wreck…everything okay?" Lizzie was her cheerful self as she opened the door.

"I'm fine, Mam…late night…that's all…" Mark looked into the front room to see his dad still sleeping. Seemed to sleep a lot these days, he'd thought to himself.

"Why don't you call by later…I'm making shepherd's pie."

Mark wished he could but he had a job that would probably have him working into the night, at times like this, he wished he'd stayed at school and got a proper education and a nine to five job.

Hindsight is a wonderful thing, he'd thought.

He had so many ties with the children and everything, and all he really wanted to do these days was to be there for his mother and support her in looking after his dad. It was hard, his heart wasn't in his work, but he had to support his family.

Turning back as he opened the gate, he smiled at his mother.

"Tell ya what, Mam…keep a bit aside for me for tomorrow…can heat it up…"

Fr Waters didn't have to be asked twice though, came down the hallway with his nose in the air.

"God bless all here…the door was open, Lizzie…goodness something smells nice…"

Lizzie was after washing the hall floor and left the door open to dry it.

"Good morning Father…come in…be careful, the floor is wet in places…I'm only after washing it…come in…there's plenty in it…"

He sat at the table and after second helpings he complimented her on the best shepherd's pie he had ever eaten.

He sat with Francis for a while, shook his head on his way out and he was off. Lizzie knew he was failing a little bit every day, she could see it herself, but if someone called who hadn't seen him for a while, she could nearly see the shock on their faces. Of late there was a constant dribble going down one side of his mouth, she would keep a damp face cloth nearby to wipe it, but it was beginning to leave a trace.

It had been a good night with him, he'd slept well and she was so grateful for the company of Sophia, a qualified nurse, a very strong-looking girl, not far off six-foot, Lizzie thought. So kind and caring, had stuck her head in a few times during the night to see if everything was okay. It was so nice having the company, Lizzie thought she couldn't expect Elizabeth or Mark to step in at night, they both had very young families, but if truth be known, she was beginning to feel the strain.

The loneliness was getting to her, she was becoming a bit scared of being on her own, not scared of Francis, just scared of maybe losing him in the night. She'd had thoughts of dread of late.

As she washed his face and hands, like she'd done every morning, Lizzie noticed the skin on his face had gotten very dry. He'd sit motionless staring at her, except for the occasional lifting of his right hand to gently scratch his face. Twirling the quilt with two fingers of his left hand.

"My darling, Francis…are you okay, my love? I wish…"

She put her arms around her husband and cried aloud, and so did he. Nobody around, they shared their sadness and she held him tight until the moment had passed. She knew her Francis was still in there, she just knew he was.

All cleaned up and refreshed after the night, he fell asleep in her arms.

There were plenty of daily chores to be done but they would wait, she would hold him tight and warm his heart. That heart of gold that cared so much for everyone, that gave until there was no more to give, that was now trapped in this rigid body, unrecognisable to her at times.

He was a shadow of his former self, his bones almost visible through his disease-eaten flesh. His eyes lost and frightened-looking, his breathing laboured with the least little movement, as she looked on helplessly.

The doorbell rang, without thinking Lizzie went to answer it, leaving Francis asleep.

"I'm sorry, Lizzie…I think I might have left my…" Sophia stopped as she noticed Lizzie had been crying.

"Everything okay, Lizzie? You're upset about something? Francis okay?"

"Oh…I'm fine…just…you know…"

Sophia gave her a hug and reassured her that it was perfectly okay to cry if she wanted to, whether or not she was in a hurry Lizzie didn't know and she hadn't said, but she'd taken the time to sit and have a coffee with her and a lovely chat. *Sometimes to give off your time is the most precious gift,* she'd thought.

Mark and Elizabeth were so relieved to hear that Sofia and Lizzie had got on and she had been appreciated so much, they wondered why they hadn't done it long before, but they didn't want to upset their mother. She really was doing a great job in looking after their dad, but there comes a time!!!

Franie's school had rang the bus station looking for Tim, it was the only contact number they'd had for her parents. Elizabeth hadn't got round to giving them the house number when they got the phone in.

Franie was really upset and wanted to go home, Tim had rang home but Elizabeth had gone to her mother's house with baby Lucy.

Lizzie answered the phone and gave it to Elizabeth.

"Can you pick her up…I can't get away here I have no cover…" Tim sounded anxious. Elizabeth hurriedly put Lucy into the car and was off down the road in a flash. Lizzie had told her to leave Lucy with her but Elizabeth wouldn't hear of it, she was like a basket of cats and needed to sleep.

"Whatever's the matter?" Elizabeth leaving Lucy asleep in the car ran to the school door to find Franie sobbing on a bench inside, teacher doing her best to console her.

"I don't know what the matter is…poor Franie got so upset after playtime…we've asked her if someone upset her and she's said no…she didn't fall or anything…I'm so sorry to have to call you in, but there was no consoling her."

"…There you are now Franie…mummy's here…" The teacher walked them to the gate and waved them off.

Elizabeth thought it best to let Franie settle a bit before she asked her what had upset her. Once in the car, she stopped crying and held hands with Lucy, who looked half-asleep.

"What upset you in school Franie…" Now home and well settled, Elizabeth thought she'd better get to the bottom of this.

"Pamela said something…" Franie was playing with her doll's hair curling it round her finger.

"What did she say……?" Elizabeth was slightly worried.

"She said…" and she was off bawling again.

"Shhh…it's okay…mummy will sort it…"

It was bedtime and Franie was playing with the suds in the bath.

"C'mon young lady…bedtime…" All snuggled up in bed, Elizabeth was settling down to reading a bedtime story, Joe fast asleep and Lucy sucking her thumb, about to give in to slumber, she decided she would address the school problem again.

"Pamela said her dog Spike had gone to doggie Heaven…and I said to her that he was only having a big sleep because he was really tired…like Poppy. Remember? Remember you said Poppy might have to go for a big sleep when he gets really tired…well she said he will never wake up again…and I said he would, he was just tired…and she said I was being silly…she said nobody can wake up when they…"

Franie turned her head into the pillow and started to cry again.

Elizabeth took her in her arms and held her tight.

"It's not true…is it mummy?" She'd sobbed and Elizabeth had held her until she was sound asleep, she would have to talk to her in the morning.

Francis tried to get out of the bed, started to throw the blankets off, angrily hitting the bed head. Lizzie was cleaning out the fireplace to light a nice fire, turning to help him she tripped over the mat and hit her hand off the side of the table, it was agony.

Holding it tightly to ease the pain, she went to see Francis who seemed very agitated and angry. He took her by the wrists as he'd often done before, the pain now excruciating in her hand. Sitting on the side of the bed, she calmed him and reassured him everything would be okay. Tired after his episode, he'd given in to exhaustion and let her go.

Mark had noticed her hand when he called by later that day, it had swollen a bit but nothing to be alarmed about, Lizzie with her knowledge of injuries from years back, had just got on with the day.

"Was it, Dad?" Pointing to her hand and sipping his tea, Mark looked concerned. Lizzie explained how she'd fallen over the mat and left it at that. Mark had seen Francis in action when he'd get one of those episodes, as Lizzie would call them. He knew the strength he could have in that moment and the exhaustion that came afterwards.

There was no more said.

"How are you today, Dad?" Mark had come by especially to give his dad a shave, he wouldn't hear of the nurse doing it or anyone else for that matter. Mark had a way with him. He wondered though if it might not be a good idea, he looked so worn and tired.

"Maybe we'll do it tomorrow…eh?" He tidied the bed a bit and sat beside his dad to read a bit of the paper aloud, never sure if he was taking it in but one never knows. Lizzie passing by the room glanced in and for a moment it put her in mind of when Mark was a baby and Francis would read to him, the tables had turned she'd thought to herself.

She would have him bathed and ready for bed when Francis would come in from work and he would take him in his arms and swing him around until he was dizzy, she could still hear Mark laughing he'd had such a contagious laugh. Slow to walk Francis always made a fuss of him, he'd sit on the floor playing with him until bedtime and read to him until he'd fall asleep.

Chapter 24

Lizzie trying to keep his dinner hot would look on and laugh along. Precious memories, she'd wondered if Mark remembered any of that.

Probably not, she'd thought, he'd often spoke of Elizabeth when they were young and how she'd been a real daddy's girl which she was, but Francis was mad about the two of them, couldn't do enough.

Though Elizabeth was constantly looking for her dad's attention. Francis was looking out for the both of them, always.

She'd remembered the hour of separation, when Francis would have to travel with his work, Elizabeth would sulk and throw her tantrums the whole day through. Eventually break down and cry. She was very fond of him. As she grew older though, Lizzie watched her use that fondness to her advantage, she'd have her dad under her little finger, got everything she'd wanted to make up for his absence due to work.

Once while based at home, Francis saw through her cunning ways and put a stop to it very fast, Elizabeth retaliated all through her teenage years. Such a pity he didn't recognise the lovely person she'd now become, a loving wife, a brilliant mother and to Lizzie and her dad, a lovely daughter, too little too late for Francis but whatever had brought about that change, Lizzie was very grateful.

"There'll be no shaving Dad today, I think…" Mark took his cup to the sink and left the paper on the table. "Can I do anything for you, Mam? Do you think he looks a bit more frail today?" It had been years since she'd checked Mark for biting his nails. He'd been a devil for it as a child, looking at him now, she'd thought it was more worry and concern that made him do it.

"I don't think so love…sure he's up one day and down the next…that's the way he'll be unfortunately…go on off with you now…we're grand…" She kissed his face and walked him to the door.

Walking back to the room, she knew Mark was right Francis was failing right before their eyes, she would sit with him for a while.

"Are you okay my love?" She rubbed his chin. "You need a shave you know…" She thought she saw him smile, it made her heart leap.

The nurse was due and with her help, she would smarten him up a bit, clean clothes, a little wash, be like a new pin.

Her hand was so painful, it would be difficult to do it alone so she would wait.

"Oh dear…Lizzie, I'm so sorry…Francis has a bed sore…it's impossible to avoid them…and we're so attentive to him…"

Lizzie looked to see a patch of his back red raw. It had come over night, the skin was so fragile now that the least little movement was going to tear it. "…I'm so sorry, Lizzie…they go with the territory as you know…just, I was so happy to see him clear of them all along…poor Francis…we'll look after you…" She'd winked at Francis and went out to her car to get an ointment to treat it.

Lizzie had seen so much of this on the ward she'd nursed on way back in her nursing days, seemed like another lifetime now she knew the pain that went with them that would keep a patient awake half the night crying out for the nurse to do something. Unfortunately there was very little you could do only to make the patient as comfortable as possible and hope for healing, they were impossible to heal.

Usually, as with Francis now the patient was bedridden and the pressure of the body, often wet from being incontinent rubbing against the sheets, would be the main cause of the sores. She'd changed Francis so often aware of this, often using talcum powder to keep him dry in the night so as not to disturb him in his sleep.

But with his skin so frail and paper-like, it was impossible to avoid it now.

"My poor Francis…what's next?" Not one to look on the dark side but Lizzie was finding this harder and harder every day.

"There we are…" As the nurse came through the door, she brought a gust of wind with her. "Whew! Nearly blew away Francis…" She smiled at Lizzie and made light of the moment.

Lizzie would put her ear to Francis's mouth to hear his whisper, his voice so faint now sometimes even then she could not make out what he was saying, often she would just nod or smile at him, hoping this would please him. From what she could make out he had said, "Thanks," after the nurse had left and he was nice and comfortable.

His hand felt so cold as she took it in hers, she kissed it and put it under the quilt.

"No need for thanks…sure where else would I be but alongside you."

The fire lit and the room nice and cosy, she would take down the photo album, he'd like that she'd thought.

"A nice cup of tea…what do you think Francis…"

As she turned the pages, usually he would take over and turn them much quicker than she would, this time, he just looked on.

"Remember this Francis…remember Maisie fell into the pond and we had to fish her out…don't know who took that photo…must have been Harry…oh we laughed that day…didn't we…eh!" Lizzie thought to herself, it had been a long time since they'd had a good laugh.

Harry and Maisie were just a scream together, one more cracked than the other, but great company, they'd had many a good day out together.

As she went through the album and ranted on about the years gone by from one photo to the other, Lizzie hadn't noticed Francis had fallen asleep, she'd been talking to herself.

She would get on with the dinner and leave him to rest.

She would mash potatoes and cabbage, he'd like that, was tasty and easy to feed with the spoon, might even make some gravy.

Sometimes Francis would breathe so low that she would have to check to see that he was still breathing at all. With bated breath she would approach him and with a sigh of relief find that he was just quietly breathing. Not today, it was like a shadow hung over him, eclipsed him. He had quietly passed, as was his way in life.

Would she too stop breathing at the thought of losing him? No!!

No, that would be too easy, as is life's cruel way, she would have to face the world without him, the love of her life, her reason to live.

She huddled up to him, still warm and asked him to wait for her, she wouldn't be long. She'd whispered close into his ear and hoped he'd heard.

"The man I saw in my dad…" Mark had written a piece to read at the end of the service, Lizzie still numb, had walked around in a daze for days. It had been all a blur, Elizabeth fell to pieces and Franie had gotten all grown up in a few days.

"Don't worry mummy…everything will be okay…Poppy said…"

Elizabeth, devastated, knew she should question this but then wasn't the time. She had neither the energy nor the interest.

All the formalities dealt with Lizzie wondered how she would even want to get up in the morning, now her lovely Francis had gone.

She wished she could have gone with him, there was nothing now to keep her here, family all grown and making their own way in life, the day would come when she would become a burden on them.

Francis had been her life, there was only sadness now.

Not wanting to cause a fuss, Lizzie agreed to stay with Mark and Kitty for a few days.

“The house will be cold…we’ll go back there in a few days and sort everything out…are you okay, Mam?” Mark was so caring.

It had been a huge funeral; the house had been full of people once word went out.

All great change is preceded by chaos, Lizzie wasn’t sure where she’d heard that said but there were no truer words. It certainly was chaos and what greater change than losing your life’s partner, and your best friend. No truer words indeed.

She’d smiled with the children, appeared to be content but inside she wanted to be at home, she wanted to sit with Francis and look at the photo album, she wanted him back, she wanted him back.

Waking in the morning after another restless night, for a split second, it seemed like a bad dream, then reality would hit and the pain would come back. Not a physical pain, she didn’t hurt anywhere, just an inward surge of pain right through her body. She wanted to cry out, nothing was going to rid her of this pain of loss, nothing.

Walking up the garden path, her legs felt like jelly, it was like the ground beneath her was mushy and she was sinking. As Mark opened the door, he turned to her, “Are you sure you want to do this? There’s plenty of time…you sure you’re ready?” Looking at his mother, he could see she was anything but ready. *But are you ever ready?* he’d thought to himself. Keeping the best side out, he’d felt like he was going to burst himself sometimes, he missed his dad so much.

Lizzie walked straight into the room where she had spent so much time looking after Francis, tending to his every need and wished she could do it all over again. Sitting on his bed she took his quilt and smelled it, it still smelled of him. She held it to her heart and felt it break another little bit. Mark began to tidy around, not wanting to intrude on her thoughts, he knew their relationship was special, he'd always known that. As he grew up, he'd hoped someday he would have that himself with someone. With Kitty, he had found the love of his life but it still didn't come close to what he'd seen with his mother and father, they were something else. He couldn't explain it but what they'd had was very rare, she was lost!

"Franie…what did you mean when you said everything would be okay…that Poppy had said it?" Elizabeth had no choice but to pull herself together, she would have to grieve when the busy house had gone quiet. Franie was pulling the hair off her doll in the corner.

"And why are you doing that?" Taking the doll she asked her again.

"Poppy told me in my dream…it's easy, you just have to talk to him…he'll be listening…and I hate that doll!!!"

She stormed up the stairs to her room.

Elizabeth didn't know what to think. *Sometimes I wonder what goes on in that head,* she thought to herself and picked Lucy up off the floor where she had begun to pick up the hair of the doll and put it into her mouth, yes, she would have to do her grieving when the house was quiet.

Maybe she'd thought it's a blessing having so much to do, keeps your mind occupied, though life's journey can take us on different paths, in times of trouble, all paths lead home. She would call on her mother in the morning. She missed her dad.

Mark and Tim had come round to reorganise the sitting room, carried the bed back upstairs and took the wheelchair back to the clinic from where it had been on loan.

It had been a week since the passing of Francis and Lizzie had spent her first night alone in the house, though Mark wanted to stay to keep her company, she'd decided she might as well get used to it.

She hadn't slept a wink and it showed in her face, her eyes still bearing the signs of grief were swollen and puffy, her body fragile bearing the ache of loss. It was as if a part of her had died and what was left was struggling to go on. She felt damaged and empty, like she had stopped functioning.

Chapter 25

Mark, in an effort to raise her spirits, had suggested that they should maybe give the room a facelift.

"It's been a while since anything was done with this room, Mam...what do you think...maybe a new carpet...bit of paint...freshen it up a bit?" Lizzie knew he'd had her best interests at heart but she'd wanted everything to be left as it was, in every little corner of the room where others might see the need for redecorating Lizzie saw Francis. She could still feel his presence there, smell him almost feel him if only in her mind. She wanted to hold on to it as long as she could, the redecorating could wait.

She'd sit for hours not reading, not even thinking just being there, she'd felt closer to him in that room than anywhere else in the house.

She'd talk to him as if he were listening and sometimes she thought he was, a feeling would come over her, a comforting feeling, she couldn't explain it. People were so kind, but she didn't want kind, she wanted Francis. There were flowers sent, cakes brought to the door, even offers of money in case she was in need of it, all of this but all she'd wanted was Francis. *Is this the price you pay for having someone in your life with whom you have shared unspeakable love? Their loss so much so that you want to stop living, like something inside you dies though you still live.* Lizzie had many thoughts, it was too soon for memories, too raw. Everyone had lost someone, she'd thought to herself she wasn't the only one, she'd known that and she should have been prepared, she'd known that too. There was never going to be a different outcome, but she wouldn't allow herself to be prepared, while she had Francis, she would never think of being without him. One thing she did know was that death was the only thing that could ever part them and it had its way in the end.

As days went on and turned into weeks, she'd held on to that moment in her heart, she just could not let it go, Mark and Elizabeth were getting very concerned. They'd gone round there with the children but she'd seemed distant, she'd made the tea and chatted but not like she used to. Mark suggested maybe having a chat with her but Elizabeth was of no help at all, just the mention of her dad and she was in bits again. Mark would take her out for lunch and talk to her, but Lizzie refused to go, she hadn't been outside the house for weeks.

Hadn't washed or changed her clothes, which was so unlike her, she was always so proud of her appearance. She'd even refused to talk to Maisie, her lifelong friend.

Maisie had rang several times and gotten no answer, she would call by.

They hugged at the door and it all came out. Lizzie was holding on to her grief so tightly that the whole world had become her enemy.

Seeing Maisie brought down that wall that she had built around her, that wall of grief. She should have called round sooner but she'd thought she would have needed a bit of space with her family, maybe it's easier to talk to a friend at a time like this. Maisie wasn't sure but she would listen and be there for her as long as it took. Lizzie made the tea.

"I'm lost Maisie…I can't let it go…I miss him so much…I'm nothing without him…" With a lump in her throat Maisie comforted her friend. Looking round the kitchen, she could see there hadn't been much interest in housekeeping either.

They chatted for a while and Lizzie found herself talking about days gone by, actually talking about their memories. She didn't think she would ever be able to look back, thought she would be stuck in time forever. She had moved on without realising it, she just needed to talk.

Life would go on regardless. Francis would become a memory, she had to accept that. It was why she couldn't move on, she'd hoped that by staying in the moment of that day, she would keep him closer.

Though she'd taken a trip down memory lane with Maisie she wasn't ready yet, and she wouldn't for a long time, if ever be ready to put her Francis in the past.

When Mark called by with the paper, Lizzie had tidied up. She was looking fresh and had changed her clothes, not wanting to remark in case of embarrassing her, he kissed her and gave her a hug.

Not meaning to get upset, he was angry with himself for crying, it was like a release he'd been so worried about her.

"Sorry Mam…I'm so sorry…I thought we'd lost you too…"

Walking down the road, Lizzie felt her legs a bit like jelly, she was pushing herself, almost nervous of going out, of meeting people or maybe having to talk about Francis. What would she say? Would she be able to speak without falling to pieces? Jeffrey next door, came running out of his house, nothing said just the tightest hug she'd ever felt. In fact it was the first time she'd actually felt anything again. The numbness had subsided.

Elizabeth wondered if her mother would be up to having Franie for an hour, Mark thought it would be good for her, a bit of distraction.

He was so pleased to see she was coming round a bit and hoped she would continue to do so. Franie would keep her in chat for a while.

Lizzie was delighted to have her round, she would maybe take her to the park to feed the ducks, she felt her heart lift after coming off the phone with Elizabeth.

Full of the joys as usual, Franie was delighted to be going to the park.

"Is it far to Heaven Nanny?" Looking up at the sky, she seemed so sincere. Lizzie squeezed her hand unknowingly.

"That's too tight Nanny…" She pulled her hand away and Lizzie apologised for holding it so tight.

"…Poppy told me to look up at the sky…before I go to bed and…" Franie stopped talking for a moment then continued

"…and…I would see sparkly diamonds…is Poppy sad too?"

Lizzie thought to herself how selfish she had been all those weeks, she hadn't thought to look around her, she hadn't noticed the heartbreak that was going on. Too wrapped up in her own grief, she didn't give a thought to Mark who had lost a most wonderful father, to Elizabeth heartbroken and the children, Franie, Seanie, Alfie, Eilish, Joe and even baby

Lucy. Sure they must be missing their Poppy as much as she was. Grief could make you selfish, anger following closely in its wake.

Lizzie thought to herself as she got out of bed, sun shining through the bedroom window.

"Today, I am going to remember the good times…I am going to put my sadness to one side and remember Francis in the happy way we used to be…" Pottering around the house she thought to herself, "Maybe Mark is right…that room could do with redecorating…"

She was feeling bright and cheerful. She was dealing with this, or so she'd thought until she'd opened a drawer and a sock belonging to Francis fell out. Her whole world collapsed again, it seemed grief would be her lasting companion hard as she tried, it had a hold on her.

She would only be up and she'd be down again, she was no longer whole, would she ever be again?

Sitting in the kitchen with her cup of tea, feeling a little better, she touched the ring on her finger, never once taken off over the years she remembered like it was yesterday, the day Francis put it on.

She'd never had an engagement ring, back then one would be well to do to get an engagement ring, she'd just had her wedding ring.

All those years ago now, sometimes happy sometimes sad but always with Francis, she slid the ring off her finger to see the mark it had left.

Just a simple ring of gold but within it encased her whole life.

Francis had never worn a ring, wasn't the thing back then he used to say he didn't need gold he'd had one of life's treasures in having Lizzie.

She remembered what Franie had said in the park about the sparkly diamonds in the sky, she was so fond of her Poppy.

Lizzie wondered if maybe she would take her to visit him in the cemetery and bring some flowers. Franie was delighted to go and Lizzie was delighted to have the company. It was a lonely place, Franie had run ahead soon as they reached the gate and by the time Lizzie had caught up with her, she was deep in conversation. Either that or she was praying and Lizzie didn't think she would know that many prayers. Her facial expressions made her think she was indeed in deep conversation.

Lizzie placed the flowers with a kiss on the grave while Franie looked on. Walking away, she held her hand, and as they reached the gate of the cemetery Franie turned and waved goodbye.

"Did you have a nice chat with Poppy?" Franie looking very content was skipping along. She smiled and Lizzie wished she could once again know the innocence of childhood.

She knew she would miss Francis every day and longed to be with him, she longed to be loved again the way he had loved her. She knew she was so lucky to have a family that loved her and she would play along for as long as she had to, but life now had changed for her. So much so that she'd hoped it wouldn't be too long before she would be with her Francis again, thoughts she would have to keep to herself, inner feeling that would have no outward show.

"We watched, helplessly
As the man was stolen
Piece by piece before our eyes.
Like the hawk
That hovers over its prey.
Until finally he was consumed.
Somehow you switch off
As though in stormy waters
You go below the swell.
To quiet waters below
To ride out the storm.
Then the moment passes
As if, a silent cry.
Alzheimer's, the long goodbye."

CPSIA information can be obtained
at www.ICGtesting.com
Printed in the USA
BVHW042106210621
610137BV00012B/166

9 781528 913416